# HAPPINESS TO LIVE BY

## 100 INSPIRING STORIES TO SMILE ABOUT

## ZIG ZIGLAR

W PUBLISHING GROUP

AN IMPRINT OF THOMAS NELSON

*Happiness to Live By*

© 2022 The Zig Ziglar Corporation

Portions of this book are excerpted and adapted from *Something to Smile About* 9780840791832 © 1997 and *Something Else to Smile About* 9780849929922 © 1999.

Scripture quotations marked KJV are taken from the King James Version. Public domain.

Scripture quotations marked NKJV are taken from the New King James Version®. Copyright © 1982 by Thomas Nelson. Used by permission. All rights reserved.

Published in Nashville, Tennessee, by W Publishing, an imprint of Thomas Nelson.

Published in association with the literary agency of Literary Management Group, LLC.

Thomas Nelson titles may be purchased in bulk for educational, business, fund-raising, or sales promotional use. For information, please email SpecialMarkets@ThomasNelson.com.

Any internet addresses, phone numbers, or company or product information printed in this book are offered as a resource and are not intended in any way to be or to imply an endorsement by Thomas Nelson, nor does Thomas Nelson vouch for the existence, content, or services of these sites, phone numbers, companies, or products beyond the life of this book.

ISBN 978-0-7852-9640-9 (audiobook)
ISBN 978-0-7852-9639-3 (eBook)

Library of Congress Cataloging-in-Publication Data on File

ISBN 978-0-7852-9638-6

*Printed in the United States of America*

22  23  24  25  26    LSC    10  9  8  7  6  5  4  3  2  1

# CONTENTS

*Introduction*                                                   VII

The Power of Attitude . . . . . . . . . . . . 1

Ambition—Good or Bad? . . . . . . . . . . . 3

Don't Give It a Thought . . . . . . . . . . . 5

Let Your Reach Exceed Your Grasp . . . . . . . 7

Be Grateful for Your Problems . . . . . . . . 9

Those "Instant" Successes . . . . . . . . . . 11

Getting Out of the Box . . . . . . . . . . . 13

K.I.S.S. . . . . . . . . . . . . . . . . 15

It's Never Too Late! . . . . . . . . . . . . 17

A Team of All-Stars or an All-Star Team? . . . . . 19

Never Follow a Bad Shot with a Bad Decision . . . . 21

Get To or Got To? . . . . . . . . . . . . . 23

She Gave Everything She Had . . . . . . . . . 25

Out of the Ashes . . . . . . . . . . . . . 27

Work—Who Needs It? . . . . . . . . . . . . 29

Gossip Is Enormously Destructive . . . . . . . . 31

Miss Amy Whittington Was a Difference-Maker . . . . 33

Help Others—Help Yourself . . . . . . . . . . 35

Where Will the Records Stop? . . . . . . . . 37

Moving Up in Life . . . . . . . . . . . . . 39

Follow the Leader—If . . . . . . . . . . . . 41

Motivation, Manipulation, and Leadership. . . . . 43

Overcoming Fear . . . . . . . . . . . . . 45

Is There More Than One Way? . . . . . . . . 47

Hope in the Future . . . . . . . . . . . . 49

She Drew the Line. . . . . . . . . . . . . 51

Be Kind and Listen . . . . . . . . . . . . 53

The "Seat" of Your Attitude . . . . . . . . . 55

Concentrate on Your Responsibilities . . . . . . 57

Success Is a Partnership. . . . . . . . . . . 59

Looking for Mutually Beneficial Solutions . . . . . 61

Little Things Do Make Big Differences . . . . . . 63

Leadership That Leads . . . . . . . . . . . 65

He Got Better, Not Bitter. . . . . . . . . . . 67

It's Better to Give . . . . . . . . . . . . . 69

We're Both on the Same Side . . . . . . . . 71

Reward Yourself . . . . . . . . . . . . . 73

Persistence Really Does Pay. . . . . . . . . . 75

I'm C2 and Fat-Free . . . . . . . . . . . . 77

The Part-Timer Made It Big-Time . . . . . . . 79

Conviction Is the Key . . . . . . . . . . . . 81

A Strange Way to Show Love . . . . . . . . . 83

One Incident Can Change Us Forever . . . . . . 85

Leaders Accept Responsibility . . . . . . . . . 87

The Young Persuader . . . . . . . . . . . . 89

Those Excuses We Make . . . . . . . . . . . 91

Truth Is Stranger and More Exciting Than Fiction . . . . 93

The Ultimate Optimist . . . . . . . . . . . 95

Do Something Nice Today . . . . . . . . . 97

Three Sides to the Story . . . . . . . . . . 99

She Passed the Test—Can You? . . . . . . . . .101

Dad, You *Do* Choose Your Daughter's Husband . . . .103

That First Impression . . . . . . . . . . . .105

I'm the Only One Who Does Anything Around Here . . .107

One Basket at a Time . . . . . . . . . . . .109

Why You Are Where You Are . . . . . . . . . .111

The Window of Opportunity . . . . . . . . .113

The Heart of a Champion . . . . . . . . . . .115

Most of Us Are Parrots . . . . . . . . . . .117

Intelligent Selfishness . . . . . . . . . . . 119

The Power of the Word . . . . . . . . . . .121

A Bear in a Tree . . . . . . . . . . . . .123

What Do You Expect? . . . . . . . . . . . .125

The Edsel Was an Outstanding Success . . . . . .127

Education Is Important . . . . . . . . . . .129

Is Guilt Good or Bad? . . . . . . . . . . . .131

Grow/Swell . . . . . . . . . . . . . . .133

Try It—Maybe You Can . . . . . . . . . . .135

My Most Unforgettable Character . . . . . . . .137

Personality or Character? . . . . . . . . . .139

Handling Criticism . . . . . . . . . . . . .141

Anything Can Happen—and It Usually Does . . . . .143

Memory Is Important . . . . . . . . . . . .145

The Fully Equipped Cow . . . . . . . . . . .147

Busy but Polite. . . . . . . . . . . . . .149

A Timeless Truth . . . . . . . . . . . . .151

Why Worry? . . . . . . . . . . . . . .153

You've Failed—Now Sit Down . . . . . . . .155

Economic Need and Crime . . . . . . . . .157

Give What You've Got . . . . . . . . . . .159

The Hawk and the Sparrow . . . . . . . . .161

School Versus Finishing Education . . . . . . .163

The Responsibility Is Yours . . . . . . . . .165

This Is a Philosophy, Not a Tactic . . . . . . .167

Leave Something Behind . . . . . . . . . .169

From Wealth to Broke to Wealth. . . . . . . .171

Manners Do Matter . . . . . . . . . . .173

Keep Your Finger in the Pie . . . . . . . . .175

Turning Tragedy into Triumph . . . . . . . .177

That Is Most Unfortunate. . . . . . . . . .179

Careful What You Leave . . . . . . . . . .181

His Commitment Was Total . . . . . . . . .183

This Mother Is Right . . . . . . . . . . .185

If the Decision Is Wrong, Change It . . . . . . .187

Character Makes the Difference. . . . . . . .189

Big Events Don't Always Get Big Attention . . . . .191

Healthy Fear . . . . . . . . . . . . .193

Getting Even . . . . . . . . . . . . .195

How Old Are You? . . . . . . . . . . . .197

Needed—One More Friend . . . . . . . . .199

# INTRODUCTION

What if, in just a couple of minutes, you could experience a moment that brings you hope, possibilities, and happiness? The noise of social media and the daily news cloud our vision and dampen our spirits. The good news is you have a choice. You can choose happiness.

The secret to happiness? Somebody once asked me to pick the one thing that, more than anything else, made Dad who he was and made him more successful in every area of life. Here it is: every day, for more than five decades, he started the day by reading and learning something new, which he internalized and simplified so that he could share it with someone else for their benefit. This simple idea and action made Zig Ziglar who he was.

Here is the interesting thing. It's been said that the opposite of depression is not happiness. The opposite of depression is purpose. I have never known a happier person than Dad. Why? Because happiness is the byproduct of pursuing purpose. I believe that each of us may have a purpose that is unique to us, but I also believe that we all share a common purpose—to serve others and to be a positive influence in their lives.

Why is this book for you at this very moment? Reading just a few pages will drown out the noise and give you hope and encouragement right now. Reflecting on the simple takeaways at the end of each short story will allow you to close out the message with lightheartedness. And then, when you tell someone you care about the story you just read and you do it for their benefit, you will be moving toward your purpose—to be a difference-maker in the lives of the people who mean the most to you. The simple act of sharing and caring changes you and those you touch, and this intentional action of purpose creates the byproduct of happiness.

Start now. Go ahead. Flip the pages and read just one story that catches your eye. Think about what you read. Then text someone you care about and say, "Hey, I just read something that reminded me of you. I just wanted to tell you that I love you and care about you, and I couldn't wait to tell you." Now imagine what their reply will be. You just smiled, didn't you? Imagine doing this simple thing every day. Maybe you're in the bookstore and haven't purchased the book yet. Text someone anyway—before you buy the book—and see what happens. I dare you.

True happiness is not found in things or in circumstances. True happiness is found along the road of life when you make a difference in someone else's life.

*Tom Ziglar*

# THE POWER OF ATTITUDE

Do not end a meeting until a "who and when" to
each problem have been assigned to a specific
individual with an appropriate solution. A decision
without a deadline is a meaningless discussion.

My friend John Maxwell said, "Never underestimate the
power of your attitude. It is the advance man of our true
selves. Its roots are inward, but its fruit is outward. It is our
best friend, or our worst enemy. It is more honest and more
consistent than our words. It has an outward look based on
past experiences. It is the thing which draws people to us or
repels them. It is never content until it is expressed. It is the
librarian of our past; it's the speaker of our present, and it's
the prophet of our future."

Many people have stated that attitudes are more
important than facts, and past research established that
approximately 85 percent of the reason we get jobs and
get ahead in those jobs has to do with our attitudes.

Unfortunately, among too many of us, when someone speaks of attitude, it's invariably a reference to a bad one.

Attitude is the key to education. It's the key to getting along with others and moving ahead in life. The student with the right attitude is more than willing to study to accomplish the objective of passing a course. A worker with the right attitude will learn to do their job better and proceed cheerfully in doing that job. The husband or wife with the right attitude will handle difficult situations in a much more effective way and enhance the relationship substantially. The physician with the right attitude will have a leg up in administering care to patients.

When everything else is equal or if there is any doubt, the coach will always choose the athlete with the best attitude. So will the employer or the man or woman seeking a mate. Message: develop a winning attitude.

*When asked to clean his room, the teenager responded with feigned dismay: "What? You want me to create an imbalance in the natural ecology of my environment?"*

DOROTHEA KENT

# AMBITION—GOOD OR BAD?

*Lack of direction, not lack of time, is the problem.*
*We all have twenty-four-hour days.*

It is my conviction that ambition, fueled by compassion, wisdom, and integrity, is a powerful force for good. It will turn the wheels of industry and open the door of opportunity for you and countless thousands of other people. But fueled by greed and the lust for power, ambition is a destructive force that ultimately does irreparable damage to the individual in its grasp and to the people within its reach.

It is more than just a cliché to say that ambition can either make us or break us. It makes us when we hear the words of Henry Van Dyke, who said, "There is a loftier ambition than merely to stand high in the world. It is to stoop down and lift mankind a little higher." George Matthew Adams observed, "He climbs highest who helps another up." John Lubbock put it this way: "To do something, however small, to make others happier and better is the highest ambition, the most elevating hope, which can inspire a human being."

As a youngster in Yazoo City, Mississippi, I frequently heard my mother and the man for whom I worked in a grocery store describe an individual by saying, "He is really a very ambitious young man," or "She really has a lot of ambition." The tone of voice indicated that they were very favorably identifying one of the traits of that young person. I understood implicitly that they were talking about ambition fueled by compassion, wisdom, and integrity. On the other hand, I heard them say on numerous occasions, "He is a nice person, but he just doesn't have any ambition."

From my perspective, people who have ability—and that includes anyone reading these words—and do not use that ability represent one of the real tragedies of life. The old saying that you either "use it or lose it" is true. In a nutshell, ambition fueled with compassion and direction can be a powerful force for good.

*"It was so cold where we were," one man boasted, "that the candle froze and we couldn't blow it out." "That's nothing!" said the other. "Where we were the words came out of our mouths in little pieces of ice and we had to fry them to see what we were talking about."*

COURIER JOURNAL MAGAZINE

4

# DON'T GIVE IT A THOUGHT

How a man plays the game shows something of
his character. How he loses shows all of it.

FROSTY WESTERING, FORMER HEAD FOOTBALL COACH

The first two and a half years I was in sales, I lived in the world of peaks and valleys—with very few peaks. Every year, during the last week in August, our company had a National Booster Week when we were encouraged to do nothing but sell, sell, sell. It proved to be a life-changing experience for me.

During that first National Booster Week, after I finally hit my stride, I sold more than two and a half times as much as I had ever sold in a single week. When the week ended, I drove to Atlanta, Georgia, to spend the night with Bill Cranford, who had brought me into the business. I arrived at 3:00 a.m., and for the next two and a half hours I gave Bill all the minute details of my marvelous week—a word-by-word, nonstop description of every call I had made. Bill patiently smiled, nodded his head, and said, "That's good! That's good!"

By 5:30 a.m., I realized that I had not even asked Bill how he or his business was doing. I was terribly embarrassed. I said, "Bill, I'm sorry! I have just been talking about me. How are you doing?"

Bill, as only he could, graciously said, "Zig, don't give it a thought! As pleased as you are with your results this week, you're not nearly as proud as I am. You see, Zig, I recruited you, taught you the fundamentals, encouraged you when you were discouraged, counseled you, and watched you grow and mature. Zig, you will never know how I feel until you have experienced the joy of teaching, training, and developing someone else who does well."

In retrospect, I realize that was the beginning of the development of the concept on which I've built my life and career, namely, that you can have everything in life you want if you will just help enough other people get what they want. Give that philosophy a try. It works because it is the golden rule expressed in a different way.

*Things change. A boy came home and told his dad*
*he was second in class. Top place was won by a girl.*
*"Surely, Son," said the father, "you're not going to be*
*beaten by a mere girl." The boy replied, "Well, you see,*
*Dad, girls are not nearly as mere as they used to be."*

EXECUTIVE SPEECHWRITER NEWSLETTER

# LET YOUR REACH EXCEED YOUR GRASP

Motivation is needed to change the costume of
the dream to the work clothes of reality based
on the goals generated by the dream.

In one of our major universities, a professor of economics gave a test to his class. The test had several sections of questions, each of which contained three categories of questions. He instructed the students to choose one question from each section on the test. The first category in each section was the hardest and was worth fifty points. The second category in each section was not quite as hard and was worth forty points. The third category in each section was the easiest and was worth only thirty points.

When the students had taken the test and all the papers had been turned in, the students who had chosen the hardest questions, or the fifty-point questions, were given As. The students who had chosen the forty-point questions were given Bs, and the students choosing the thirty-point questions, or the easiest questions, were given Cs. Whether or not their answers were correct was not considered. Understandably, the students were confused and asked the professor how he had graded their exams. The professor leaned back with a smile and explained, "I wasn't testing your knowledge. I was testing your aim."

I believe it was Browning who said, "Your reach should exceed your grasp, or what's a heaven for?" Langston Hughes wrote, "Hold fast to dreams, for if dreams die, then life is like a broken-winged bird that cannot fly." Yes, we need those dreams or, if you prefer, a vision. Solomon, the wisest man who ever lived, said, "Where there is no vision, the people perish" (Proverbs 29:18 KJV). Helen Keller was asked the question, "What would be worse than being blind?" She responded that it would be infinitely worse to have 20/20 eyesight and no vision than to be blind but have that vision.

In the declining years of his life, Albert Schweitzer was asked, "How goes it with you, Dr. Schweitzer?" The aging medical missionary responded, "My eyesight grows dim, but my vision is clearer than ever."

*If you think you're too small to have an impact, try going to bed with a mosquito.*

ANITA RODDICK

# BE GRATEFUL FOR YOUR PROBLEMS

### The only way to coast is downhill.

We all frequently deal with people who complain about the trials and tribulations of their daily lives. Life seems to be one big problem for them. I would like to take a common-sense, realistic approach and address this mindset. If there were no problems on your job, then your employer would hire a much less capable person than you to do the routine things that don't require much thought. In the business world, those who are able to solve complex problems are the ones who are the most valuable to the employer.

Many times the problems or challenges we face force us to grow and become more capable. The runner who trains for the mile run in the Olympics by running downhill will have no chance of winning the medal. The runner who trains by running uphill is far more likely to develop the speed, mental toughness, and endurance needed to win the medal.

The best thing that ever happened to boxer Gene Tunney was when he broke both hands in the ring. His manager felt that he could never again punch hard enough to be the heavyweight champion. Instead, Tunney decided that he would become a scientific boxer and win the title as a boxer, not a slugger. Boxing historians will tell you that he developed into one of the best boxers who ever fought. They will also tell you that as a puncher, he would not have had a chance against Jack Dempsey, who was considered by many to be the hardest hitter in heavyweight history. Tunney would never have been champion had he not had the problem of his broken hands.

Message: the next time you encounter a difficult climb, obstacle, or problem, you should smile and say, "Here's my chance to grow."

*The fact that there are a lot of habitual gamblers in this world proves one thing: men and women are the only animals that can be skinned more than once.*

# THOSE "INSTANT" SUCCESSES

Those who stand out from the crowd have learned
that all development is self-development.

Many times an unknown person does something spectacular and suddenly becomes a hero, a public figure, an
overnight success, the object of much envy. Let's explore this
"overnight success" syndrome, which almost always occurs
over time.

In 1979 Gerry Spiess from White Bear Lake, Minnesota,
did an incredible thing. He sailed his ten-foot boat across
the Atlantic Ocean in just fifty-four days. Most of us can
only imagine what he endured to complete his fifty-four-day
ordeal, but suddenly the whole world knew who he was.

What is the real story? Did he just have a good idea,
implement it, and "luck" into celebrity status? Gary worked,
planned, sacrificed, and studied for three years to build his
boat. He committed not only his money but also 100 percent
of his spare time for three solid years. He had to chart his

course and plan every detail, including maximum use of his space to carry the proper food, clothing, and water.

Once the trip began, so did the danger. The most dangerous and difficult part was fighting the violent seas of the Atlantic Ocean. The seas often combined with a driving, bitterly cold rain, which chilled him to the bone. By the time Gerry reached England, he was so brutally battered by the cruel sea that his entire body was black and blue. Yes, he had his day in the sun, but it's safe to say that he sacrificed and worked to receive his rewards.

Most of us are not interested in doing anything of that nature, but it's safe to say that if we're going to accomplish anything of significance, and particularly if we're going to maintain that significance, long hours of planning and even more hours of hard work are required. It's also safe to say that it's worth it because the effort is temporary, but the satisfaction and rewards can be long lasting.

*A man loaned his best friend $5,000 for plastic surgery. Unfortunately, he will never recover it because now he can't recognize him.*

# GETTING OUT OF THE BOX

It is not the brains that matter most, but that
which guides them—the character, the heart,
generous qualities, progressive ideas.

FYODOR DOSTOEVSKY

Many people set low ceilings on their expectations and capabilities. In the process, they place themselves in a "box." Alexander Wortley took that a step further and literally lived in a box. It was a mini-trailer: three feet wide, four feet long, and five feet high. He lived there until he died at the age of eighty. His box was made of wood, had a metal roof, and it housed him and all his meager belongings. Regardless of where he worked, Wortley chose to spend his life in that cramped space, even though larger, more comfortable quarters were always available.

Few of us live in a box. However, too many of us have a tendency to box ourselves in and continue to do things one way because we've "always done it this way." In many cases, time and experience have proved that "this way" is the best way. However, I challenge you to periodically take a long walk or quietly sit and think about the way you do things. Ask yourself if there might not be a better way. Could your procedures be simplified? Are they necessary at all? Could they be done more cheaply or efficiently? Could your product be longer? Shorter? A different shape? Another fabric? Another color? Sometimes you can come up with simple ideas that make a big difference. Incidentally, one advantage of a way of life that includes continual personal growth and education is that the broader and deeper your knowledge base, the more creative your problem-solving approach to life.

Simple example: For years men's coats had an inside pocket only on the right where pens and other items were kept. One day somebody had a thought: since most men are right-handed, why not put a pocket on the inside left so that they could reach in, extract the pen with their right hand, and begin writing? Not monumental, but it saves a second or two and it's sold lots of suits.

*In an election year we should not be surprised*
*the air is filled with speeches and vice versa.*

POLITICAL SPEECHWRITER JOSEPH NOLAN

# K.I.S.S.

Two sure ways to fail: think and never do, or do and never think.

When I started my sales career, one of the first things I was taught was to "Keep It Simple, Salesman." Communicate in such a way that your message is unmistakably clear. If the message is not clear, the prospect ends up confused, and a confused person seldom takes action.

This advice can be followed in any field of endeavor. For example, in marathon running today we use sports psychologists, computerized training regimens, and state-of-the-art running shoes. Perhaps all of that is necessary if you want to win the big race. I'm not denying these things help, but Toshihiko Seko didn't need them.

I was tremendously impressed when Seko won the Boston Marathon in 1981. His training program was simplicity itself, and Seko explained it with twelve words: "I run ten kilometers in the morning and twenty in the evening." At this point you probably think, *There's a catch!* But this plan enabled him to outrun the world's greatest, fastest, most gifted runners. When Seko was told that his plan seemed too simple compared to that of other marathoners, he replied, "The plan is simple, but I do it every single day, 365 days a year." Simple? Yes. Easy? No.

It is my conviction that most people fail to reach their goals not because their plans are too simple or too complicated. Most people don't reach their goals because they're not committed and willing to follow their plans.

Many of our goals do not require detailed plans, but all of them require that we follow the plan we have. Seko's plan was effective because he followed it every day. You can't get more simple than that! Follow Toshihiko Seko's example; make certain your plan to reach your goal is simple, then follow it carefully.

*Recorded on a department store voice mail: "If you are calling to place an order, press 5. If you are calling to register a complaint, press 6-4-5-9-8-3-4-8-2-2-9-5-3-9-2. Have a good day."*

# IT'S NEVER TOO LATE!

*The ladder of life is full of splinters, but you never realize it until you slide down.*

In May of 1983, Helen Hill, age ninety-five, received her high school diploma. She was absolutely ecstatic. When she finished high school seventy-six years earlier, she and her five classmates did not receive formal diplomas because the school was so much in debt that it could not afford them. Mrs. Hill was the only surviving member of the class of 1907, so she could not share her joy and excitement with her former classmates. The message is clear: A disappointment of yesterday can turn into a delight for today. It's never too late!

Carl Carson, at the tender age of sixty-four, decided to make a career change. At that age, most people think in terms of retirement, which is unfortunate. Many sixty-four-year-olds have active years left and have accumulated experiences on which they can build exciting and rewarding careers. Carson had been successful as a car and truck leasing agent. For his new career, he decided to go into the consulting business. His original plan was to sell his services to ten clients. Like many of us, when he reached his rather modest goal, he decided to do more. He began putting out a monthly newspaper, advising twelve hundred paying subscribers. By age seventy-five, Carson was crisscrossing the nation a hundred times a year, speaking at conventions and having a very good time.

The message is absolutely clear: it's never too late to dream, to learn, or to change. Too many people come up with excuses for not reaching their goals. They don't live in the right place, are too old or too young, or have a host of other excuses. I'm not saying that it's going to be easy—life is tough, but it can be rewarding! It's true that you can't stop the calendar or turn back the clock, but you can still dream, set positive goals, and use your unique abilities.

*Show me a man who walks with his head held high, and I'll show you a man who hasn't quite gotten used to his bifocals.*

*STRIPPED GEARS*

# A TEAM OF ALL-STARS OR AN ALL-STAR TEAM?

People have a way of becoming what you encourage
them to be—not what you nag them to be.

SCUDDER N. PARKER

While in Sydney, Australia, my wife and I had an opportunity to attend a performance of the Sydney Orchestra at
the famed Opera House. The seats were choice, and our
night was free, so we jumped at the opportunity. When we
arrived thirty minutes early, the orchestra members were
already warming up. The individuals came in all sizes, ages,
and ethnicities. Some of them, such as the cymbalist, would
perform five or six seconds during the entire evening, while
the cellist had one part that would extend more than twenty
minutes. As they warmed up, the music sounded like noise
to me.

At one minute before eight the conductor walked onto
the stage. Immediately, everybody sat up straight. As he

stepped onto the riser, everybody came to attention. At eight o'clock he raised the baton, and when his arms came down, the music started. What had been noise a few seconds earlier became a beautiful melody.

The orchestra leader had converted a team of all-stars to an all-star team. Although each instrument produced entirely different tones, they all blended together in harmony. No one instrument dominated any other; rather, each harmonized with and became a part of the others. Can you imagine what the results would have been had every artist made up their mind that their instrument should be the star of the performance?

The conductor had, for a number of years, been a musician in an orchestra. He had learned to be obedient and follow the orchestra conductor when he was a performer. In short, he had learned to obey so that later he could command. I once saw a young man with a T-shirt emblem proclaiming, "I follow no one." What a tragedy! Because until he learns to follow, he will never be able to lead.

*A small child pointed to a picture and asked the policeman if it really was the picture of the most-wanted person. "Yes," answered the policeman. "Well," inquired the youngster, "why didn't you keep him when you took his picture?"*

*THE ROTARIAN*

# NEVER FOLLOW A BAD SHOT
# WITH A BAD DECISION

Great fear will always lose out to great faith.

As an avid golfer I'm often puzzled by the actions of the typical high-handicap golfer. He steps up to the tee box with driver in hand, takes his stance, thinks the shot through, and hits the ball about 210 yards out and about 40 yards to the right, where it lands in the midst of some trees. He walks or rides to the ball, looks at the six-foot opening, and determines that all he's got to do to reach the green is hit the ball 175 yards through that opening, send it over the lake, and fade it over the bunker to land on the green.

Let me remind you of the scenario: He just missed a fairway roughly sixty yards wide with the ball teed up and in perfect position. For his second shot he believes he can go through a six-foot opening and make the ball act as it does when one of the top touring pros on the PGA hits it. With a confidence that generally accompanies ignorance, he steps up, fires away, and hits the ball into the lake. In anger and disgust, he then hits the ball over the green into a sand bunker. Two strokes later he is on the green, where he two-putts for a disastrous quadruple-bogey-8. He followed a bad shot with a bad decision and it cost him.

Too often all of us hit a "bad shot" (e.g., make a mistake, handle the truth loosely). Then we compound that "bad shot" by denying it, defending it, lying about it, or rationalizing it instead of quietly thinking it through, acknowledging the mistake, and working through it in a logical, forthright manner.

*As the stock market joke goes about your investments,*
*the broker makes money, the broker's firm makes*
*money, and two out of three's not bad.*

# GET TO OR GOT TO?

What we see depends mainly on what we look for.

JOHN LUBBOCK

Every morning for several years, promptly at 10:00 a.m., a prominent businesswoman visited her mother in a nursing home. She was close to her mother and loved her very much. Often she had requests for appointments at that time of day. Her response was always the same: "No, I've got to visit with my mother." Eventually, her mother died. Shortly thereafter someone asked the woman for an appointment at 10:00 a.m. It suddenly hit her that she could no longer visit her mother. Her next thought was, *Oh, I wish I could visit my mother just one more time.* From that moment on, she changed her "got to's" to "get to's."

Her story makes us realize that pleasurable things are "get to's." I get to play golf today, or I get to go on a vacation this week. Burdensome things are "got to's." I've got to go to work at 7:00 a.m. tomorrow, or I've got to clean house. Since perceptions influence thinking and performance, try this. Instead of saying, "I've got to go to work," think about people who have no job. Then you can enthusiastically change it to, "I get to go to work tomorrow." If somebody invites you to go fishing, instead of saying, "No, I've got to go to my child's game on Saturday," think about the fact that someday your child will grow up and you won't be able to go to their games. Then it's easy to change it to "get to."

It's amazing what the change in words will eventually do for your attitude. You'll find yourself looking forward to doing those things instead of feeling as if you *have* to do them. With a difference in attitude, there will be a difference in performance. With a difference in performance, there will be a difference in rewards. So think about these things, and change your "got to's" to "get to's."

*From a book critique: "I've seen better writing on the side of a Shredded Wheat box."*

STEPHANIE MANSFIELD IN THE *WASHINGTON POST*

# SHE GAVE EVERYTHING SHE HAD

The fruit we grow in the valleys of despair is
the food we will eat on the mountaintop.

FRED SMITH

Italian conductor Arturo Toscanini said that American contralto Marian Anderson had the sweetest voice "this side of heaven." She sang before royalty and heads of governments in the opera houses of Europe and America. She had an extraordinary vocal range, going from soprano to the lowest contralto with a pure tone.

Marian Anderson got her start by scrubbing floors for ten cents an hour so that she could buy a pawnshop violin. The church she attended recognized her rare talent and raised money for a professional voice teacher to work with her. When the teacher pronounced her ready, she went to New York, where critics crucified her. She returned home to regroup. Her mother and her church encouraged her and paid for more lessons.

The next time, because of the intense racial prejudice in America, she went to Europe and took the continent by storm. She came back to America and sang at the Lincoln Memorial with more than sixty thousand people in attendance. She sang "O Mia Fernando," "Ave Maria," "Gospel Train," "Trampin'," and "My Soul Is Anchored in the Lord," among other songs. Those who were privileged to hear both her singing and Martin Luther King Jr. giving his "I Have a Dream" speech say that her music was even more moving than his oratory.

One day a reporter asked her what the most satisfying moment in her life was. Without hesitation, she responded that her most satisfying moment came when she was able to tell her mother that she did not have to take in any more washing. Her honors were too numerous to mention, and yet that was her most satisfying moment. The reporter asked her, "What did your mother give you?" Marian Anderson responded, "Everything she had."

That's greatness, and giving everything we have is our key to greatness.

*The first and last completely accurate weather forecast was when God told Noah that it was going to rain.*

# OUT OF THE ASHES

*Problems produce patience; patience produces persistence; persistence produces character; character produces hope; hope produces power.*

Many times disasters or tragedies spawn incredible accomplishments and enormous progress. A tornado in August of 1883 devastated Rochester, Minnesota, and yet from those ashes came the world-famous Mayo Clinic. According to Daniel J. Murphy, in an article in *Investors Daily*, "Mother Alfred Moes, the founder of the Sisters of St. Francis, brought her untrained nuns to assist in nursing those who had been injured in the tornado. While there, she convinced the leading town doctor to head an unbuilt hospital she would raise funds to construct. That physician and surgeon's name was William Worrall Mayo and the hospital, St. Mary's, was forerunner to and still affiliated with the world-famous Mayo Clinic."

In the early part of the twentieth century, the boll weevil

devastated Southern cotton crops, hitting particularly hard in southern Alabama. The disaster was a wake-up call for the need to diversify. The farmers of that area started raising peanuts, soybeans, corn, sorghum, fresh vegetables, and more. The economy improved so much that the residents of Enterprise, Alabama, actually built a monument to the boll weevil in the center of town.

In my life a seeming disaster was a blessing in disguise. I was quickly approaching the publication date for my first book, *See You at the Top*, when my gallbladder ruptured. Because I was unable to travel, my heavy speaking schedule came to an abrupt halt for twenty-two days. During nineteen of those twenty-two days, I was able to work ten to twelve hours a day while lying in bed or sitting quietly in a chair. Had I not had those hours, the book definitely would not have met the deadline.

Message: When disaster strikes, ask, What good can come of it? In many cases you'll discover that a temporary disaster can turn into long-term gain.

*God made man. Then He stepped back,*
*looked him over, and said, "I can do better*
*than that," and He made woman.*

MARY CROWLEY

# WORK–WHO NEEDS IT?

To change your friends, family, and lifestyle,
you must first change yourself.

Somebody once said that work is the father of success and integrity is the mother. If you can get along with these two members of the family, the rest of the family will be easy to deal with. However, too many people don't make enough effort to get along with the father and leave the mother out completely. Some even quit looking for work as soon as they find a job.

Many people's concept of work is that it should be fun and meaningful, or we shouldn't be expected to do it. I'm convinced that the sheer love of work, with all its rewards, should provide enormous satisfaction. Charles Gow contends that work gives you an appetite for your meals; it lends solidity to your slumber; it gives you a perfect appreciation of a holiday. The truth is, we all need work.

Personally, I don't believe anyone enjoys what he does

any more than I enjoy what I do, and yet certain phases of my work are tedious: constant deadlines and occasional canceled or delayed flights when I just sit in an airport or on a runway for hours, for example. These things aren't fun and meaningful, but they are part of the package of what I do, so I respond when flights are delayed and use the time for research and writing.

Voltaire said that work keeps us from three great evils: boredom, vice, and poverty. With that concept in mind we can look at the benefits and understand that you don't "pay the price"—you enjoy the benefits. Thomas Edison said, "There is no substitute for hard work. Genius is one percent inspiration and ninety-nine percent perspiration." Benjamin Franklin put it this way: "The used key is always bright." And finally, Richard Cumberland observed, "It is better to wear out than to rust out."

Bottom line: Unless you work, you will miss out on many of the joys and benefits of life itself. So concentrate on the things you like about your job and its benefits. Give your job that extra burst of energy you always have on the day before vacation. You will not only enjoy your work more but *raise* and *praise* will also come your way.

*Don't overdo this work thing. Remember that the man who is always busy as a bee might awaken to discover that someone has swiped his honey.*

# GOSSIP IS ENORMOUSLY DESTRUCTIVE

## Warm hearts seldom produce hot heads.

We frequently hear little jokes about gossip, like the two people who were talking and one said, "I can't tell you any more. I've already told you more than I heard." In that line is much of the tragedy about gossip, which often destroys a person's reputation. Gossip always damages relationships, specifically with the person you are gossiping about. For example, once you have said something unkind about a person, you will feel uncomfortable around them and your relationship with them will suffer.

Dr. Adrian Rogers wisely pointed out that before we disseminate information that might be considered gossip, we must carefully ponder three issues:

1. Is it the truth? If it fails the first test, then it is not repeatable.

2. Even if it is the truth, do you really need to share it? Will it help anyone? Will it hurt anyone? Would it be better left unsaid? If there are no benefits to anyone, then what possible purpose could repeating it serve?
3. Is it kind? In our world so full of cynicism and skepticism, will repeating this story be kind? Would it be better left unsaid? Would you really be better off repeating this information?

When you analyze it this way, your chances of being a gossip are dramatically reduced. And when you consider the benefits of stopping gossip in its tracks, you'll discover they're substantial. First, you do not damage yourself, which means that your reputation and esteem are untarnished. That's good. Second, you won't harm someone else's reputation. This means that your circle of friends will be larger. Since most of us do not have any friends we would like to lose, that's good!

*A class reunion has been defined as an occasion when you meet people who used to be the same age as you.*

# MISS AMY WHITTINGTON WAS A DIFFERENCE-MAKER

*How vain it is to sit down to write when you have not stood up to live.*

HENRY DAVID THOREAU

In our lifetime, each of us influences—both by word and by deed, either for good or for bad—countless people. That means all of us are difference-makers.

Miss Amy Whittington certainly qualified as one who directly and indirectly influenced thousands of people. At age eighty-three, she was still teaching a Sunday school class in Sault Sainte Marie, Michigan. She learned that the Moody Bible Institute in Chicago was offering a seminar to teach people how to be more effective teachers. She literally saved her pennies until she had the necessary money to buy a bus ticket to Chicago. She rode the bus all night to attend the seminar to learn new methods and procedures so she could do a better job.

One of the professors, impressed with her age, enthusiasm, and the fact that she had ridden the bus all night to attend the seminar, engaged her in conversation. He asked her what age group she taught and how many were in her class. When she responded that she taught a class of junior high school boys and there were thirteen in the class, the professor asked how many kids belonged to the church. Miss Whittington replied, "Fifty." The professor, astonished that she taught more than 25 percent of the church youth, responded, "With that kind of record we should have you teach us how to teach." How right he was!

I hasten to add that people who are already good at what they do are far more likely to work at getting better than those who are marginal performers. What kind of impact did Miss Amy Whittington have? Eighty-six of those boys she taught in her Sunday school class through the years ended up in the ministry. Can you just imagine the thousands of people she directly and indirectly affected for good? She truly was a difference-maker. You are, too, so make it a good difference.

*When a man gets too big for his britches, he will find somebody else in his shoes.*

# HELP OTHERS—HELP YOURSELF

Christ said, "He who would become the greatest
among you must become the servant of all."

Somebody once made the observation that the person who is wrapped up entirely in himself makes a very small package—and the package contains an unhappy person. Think about this: Have you ever known a genuinely happy, self-centered person?

I love the story, often told, about a man who was hiking in the mountains. He was taken by surprise in a sudden snowstorm and quickly lost his way. He knew he needed to find shelter fast, or he would freeze to death. Despite all of his efforts, his hands and feet quickly went numb. In his wandering he literally tripped over another man, who was almost frozen. The hiker had to make a decision: Should he help the man, or should he continue in hopes of saving himself?

In an instant he made a decision and threw off his wet

gloves. He knelt beside the man and began massaging his arms and legs. After the hiker had worked for a few minutes, the man began to respond and was soon able to get on his feet. Together the two men, supporting each other, found help. The hiker was later informed that by helping another, he had helped himself. His numbness vanished while he was massaging the stranger's arms and legs. His heightened activity had enhanced his circulation and brought warmth to his hands and feet.

It's ironic but not surprising that when the hiker lost sight of himself and his predicament and focused on someone else, he solved his own problem. It's my conviction that the only way to reach the mountain peaks of life is to forget about self and help other people reach greater heights.

*Strange how percentages work out. We've met two hundred people who have had their fenders smashed in parking lots, but never one that's smashed anybody else's.*

BILL VAUGHN

# WHERE WILL THE RECORDS STOP?

Success is not measured by what a man accomplishes, but by the opposition he has encountered and the courage with which he has maintained the struggle against overwhelming odds.

ORISON SWETT MARDEN

In 1954 Roger Bannister ran a sub-four-minute mile and it ignited the athletic world. In 1994 Eamonn Coghlan of Ireland, at age forty-one, ran a sub-four-minute mile. Incredibly enough, Kip Keino of Ethiopia, at age fifty-five, ran a mile in four minutes and six seconds.

By 1954 more than fifty medical journals had published articles saying that the four-minute mile was not humanly possible. Doctors were warning athletes of the dire consequences to anyone who broke that "unbreakable" barrier. In the meantime coaches all over the world, with stopwatches in hand, were encouraging their charges to do their best—but to forget about breaking the "impossible" four-minute barrier.

Roger Bannister broke the barrier and changed that thinking by his performance. He refused to believe what others were saying because he didn't want to limit his own potential. His breakthrough proved that the barrier was psychological, not physiological. Years ago in *Runner's World* magazine, Jerry Lynch, PhD, said that when you believe and think you can, you activate your motivation, commitment, confidence, concentration, and excitement, all of which relate directly to achievement. On the other hand, "Whether you think you can or think you can't, you're right in both cases."

Dr. Lynch said that the path to personal excellence is cluttered with obstacles. It is my personal conviction that you can't develop your full potential without encountering serious obstacles along the way. Dr. Lynch also said that you can't stretch your limits without encountering some rough moments. You need to understand that failure and losses are acceptable learning experiences that can help improve your performance. This is true in every part of life, whether it involves athletics, academic achievement, business, or sales success. It's true that airplanes and kites rise fastest when they fly into the wind. Individuals grow stronger physically, mentally, and spiritually when they are tested with resistance or opposition.

*As legendary Green Bay Packers coach Vince Lombardi used to say about his team, "Careful. You're playing with live ammunition!"*

# MOVING UP IN LIFE

There is a lot of difference between a wise man and smart guy.

Someone accurately stated that when you hire others smarter than yourself, you prove you are smarter than they are. We apply that to all areas of ability. The sales manager should strive diligently to hire salespeople who are better at selling. That way they can share information, and they will all be even more effective. Also, by continuing to learn from each salesperson, the manager will stay one step ahead of all of them. Exactly the same thing applies in coaching. A good head coach seeks assistant coaches who know more about their specialty than he does and he learns from them. Ditto for managers in manufacturing, engineering, architecture, and other fields.

Many years ago Lawrence Welk hired an accordionist named Myron Floren. He was considered the best in his profession. When Mr. Welk told his business manager what he had done, this business manager was furious. He felt one accordion in the orchestra was enough. Mr. Welk just smiled and said the hiring was firm. The first night the business manager heard Myron play in the orchestra with Lawrence Welk, he told Mr. Welk that the new accordion player was better than he was. Lawrence Welk smiled and confided, "That's the only kind of musician I hire." That's the best way to become a success. That also helps explain one of the reasons Mr. Welk and his Champagne Music spanned four generations of music lovers. Excellence and the commitment to bring customers the best possible product are the predictors of long-term success.

All of us can learn and benefit from the knowledge and talents of others. Don't be intimidated by someone with a more successful résumé, and don't feel superior to someone who has enjoyed less success than you have. Learn from both of them.

*The boss read the notes in the Suggestion Box and complained that he wished the employees had been more specific. "What kind of kite? Which lake?"*

AMERICAN LEGION MAGAZINE

# FOLLOW THE LEADER—IF

*Experience is a hard teacher because she gives
the test first, the lesson afterwards.*

VERN LAW

I'll be the first to admit that sheep are not the most intelligent creatures on earth, but from time to time I wonder about some of us people. When sheepherders wish to move their flock from one pasture to another, if there is a slight obstacle in the path, they let a goat lead the way, and it will be the first to jump over the obstacle. The sheep follow dutifully. Interestingly enough, you could remove the obstacle, and the sheep would continue to jump over an obstacle that no longer exists.

To a degree, people are the same way. A major cross-country race in Kuala Lumpur, Malaysia, was to cover a seven-mile course. Two hours after the race began, there were no runners in sight, and the officials became concerned that something had happened. They set out in their automobiles to find the runners and discovered that all were six or more miles away, running in the wrong direction. A. J. Rogers, a race official, said the mix-up apparently occurred when the runner leading the pack took a wrong turn at the fifth checkpoint and the rest followed him.

Experts say that in a lifetime the average person directly or indirectly influences ten thousand other people. Those who are in leadership positions influence many, many more. That's the reason leadership carries such an incredible responsibility—namely, that of making certain you're heading in the right direction, that the decisions you make are character-based, and the route you choose is a good one. When you make a decision, that decision is going to influence countless other people directly or indirectly. Right decisions by the right people can influence people positively, so make good decisions.

*You'll never get ahead of anyone as long*
*as you try to get even with him.*

LOU HOLTZ

# MOTIVATION, MANIPULATION, AND LEADERSHIP

A fair-weather friend is always there when he needs you.

The word *motivation* is often confused with *manipulation*. Motivation occurs when you persuade others to take an action in their own best interests. Things such as people doing their homework, accepting responsibility for their performance, and finishing their education are the results of motivation. Manipulation is persuading others to take an action that is primarily for your benefit. Things such as selling an inferior product at an inflated price and working people overtime with no extra pay are examples of manipulation.

Manipulation self-destructs the individual doing the manipulating. Word gets out on manipulators, and people grow less and less likely to respond in a positive manner to their manipulation. Productivity declines.

Leadership occurs when you persuade a person to take

an action that is in your mutual best interests. Dwight D. Eisenhower said that leadership was the ability to persuade someone to do what you wanted him to do because he wanted to do it. When that happens, performance improves, productivity increases, and both parties win.

Comparing motivation to manipulation is like comparing kindness to deceit. The difference is the intent of the person. Motivation will cause people to act out of free choice and desire, while manipulation often results in forced compliance. One is ethical and long-lasting; the other is unethical and temporary.

Thomas Carlyle said, "A great man shows his greatness by the way he treats the little man." The value you place on people determines whether you are a motivator or a manipulator. Motivation is moving together for mutual advantage. Manipulation is persuading or even subtly coercing people to do something so that you win and they lose. With the motivator, everybody wins; with the manipulator, only the manipulator wins. And to that I might add that the victory is temporary and the price is prohibitive.

Leaders and motivators are winners; manipulators are losers who produce resentment and discord. Become a motivator; lead your people, and don't manipulate them.

*Overheard: "I spend a lot of money . . . but*
*name me one other extravagance!"*

# OVERCOMING FEAR

*Fear is the darkroom where negatives are developed.*

Fear has been correctly identified with the acrostic, False Evidence Appearing Real. The truth is that if we think something is to be feared, that perception becomes the cruelest form of reality.

A second-grade boy was overheard saying, "It's easy to be brave when you're not scared." By the same token, it's easy to talk about how to overcome fear when you have little to be afraid of. Fear is certainly real for most people, and all of us face a fear of something—maybe it's poverty, divorce, rejection, death, failure, speaking in public, or being laughed at.

How do we overcome fear? First we must learn to examine our fears. Giving a speech is the number one fear in our country, according to *Reader's Digest*. (It's also a tremendous confidence builder.) If that's your fear, ask yourself a few questions: Why am I afraid to make a speech? Is it because I'm afraid of being rejected? If so, do I think I'll be rejected? Do I believe what I'm about to say? Is my speech worth giving? Am I proud of the comments I'm about to make? As you ask yourself these questions, the fear will begin to subside. It subsides because you have explored your subconscious mind with your questions and flushed out some of your fears.

My research indicates that only three people have died while making a speech. Since more than twelve billion people have lived and only three of them died making a speech, I'd say it's a fairly safe thing to do. If you're a little nervous, consider this: You could lead a mule into a crowded room and he would be so calm that he would almost go to sleep standing up. A thoroughbred in the same situation would be as nervous as a cat. If you're a little nervous, just be grateful you're a thoroughbred—not a mule. So face those inner feelings, stand up, and speak with confidence.

*A frog telephones a psychic hotline and is told,*
*"You're going to meet a beautiful young girl who*
*will want to know everything about you." "Great!"*
*says the frog. "Will I meet her at a party?" "No,"*
*said the psychic, "next year in biology class."*

# IS THERE MORE THAN ONE WAY?

Failure is not necessarily at the end of
the road. Many times it is the beginning
of a new and more exciting trip.

One morning on my way to work, I spotted my daughter Suzan in my rearview mirror as I was driving to the office. Suzan worked closely with me on my newspaper column, and she, too, was headed for the office. A minute later she drove past me because she was in the fast-moving center lane, while I was in the slow-moving right lane. After a short while I passed her, waving and smiling as I did so. A few blocks later she passed me again. She was grinning quite broadly as if to say, "You see, Dad, the center lane is best after all." But her triumph was short-lived; in a few more blocks I passed her.

By then we were just a few blocks from the office, and traffic was considerably heavier. Suzan missed her turn and sped past me as I turned to head for the office. Just as I pulled into my parking place, Suzan—who had taken the longer but quicker route—was pulling into hers.

The first point is we really should not be too concerned when somebody gets ahead of us, whether in traffic or in life. In the ever-changing landscape of life, the sun often shines on one person for a spell, then shines on another. The second point is sometimes the shortest or easiest way is not necessarily the best or even the fastest way. We must frequently make detours to arrive at our destination. Had Suzan attempted to turn from the center lane, it might have meant disaster. Because she was flexible and willing to detour, she arrived exactly as she had planned. The third point is we should be willing and excited to learn from the success of others. If someone is able to pass us by and arrive ahead of us, we should say, "Super good! How'd you do it?" Think about it.

*Giving Congress a pay raise is like giving the captain of the Titanic a salary increase after he hit the iceberg.*

DAVID EVANS

# HOPE IN THE FUTURE

Things turn out best for the people who make
the best of the way things turn out.

JOHN WOODEN

Dr. John Maxwell says that if there's hope in the future, there's power in the present. The reason is simple: hope in the future has a dramatic impact on your thinking today. Your thinking today determines your performance today, and your performance today has a direct bearing on your future. Dr. Tony Campolo, of Eastern University in Pennsylvania, says that your past is important because it brought you to where you are, but as important as your past is, it is not nearly as important as the way you see your future. He is saying, "I understand the problems of your past. I know that you were abused as a child, raised by alcoholic parents, suffered through bankruptcy, depression, and/or alcoholism. You've gone through one or more divorces.

All of these things are traumatic events that affect the way you think and the way you act." In no way is Dr. Campolo denying any of the impact of your past, because many of those events are extremely significant. However, he is saying that despite all these things, the way you see your future is even more important.

John Johnson, the former publisher and owner of *Ebony* magazine and one of the wealthiest men in America during his lifetime, said that "men and women are limited not by the place of their birth, not by the color of their skin, but by the size of their hope."

Make friends with your past so you can focus on today, which will make your tomorrows even better. If you are familiar with my material, you realize that my nature is that of an optimist—I just can't see any point in being pessimistic. I'm not talking about denial of reality; what I am talking about is facing reality, but facing it in an optimistic way.

*It may be true that most people can't handle prosperity, but it is also true that most people don't have to.*

# SHE DREW THE LINE

*If you believe—really believe—you will persist.*

You've probably never heard of Dr. June McCarroll, but she is one of the women who truly left a mark on the world. Born in Nebraska, she was a general practitioner who lived in California. Interestingly enough, her claim to fame lies outside the world of medicine. An accident was the trigger that got her thinking about making our highways safer. Her car was side-swiped, and she determined to do something about cars that crowded others off the road.

As she was driving along a road that bulged down its center, she noticed that the bulge helped to keep motorists on their own side of the road. That gave her an idea, and she started trying to persuade the town council to "paint a line down the middle of the road" to set an example and "lead the nation in public safety." She got the typical bureaucratic response that her idea was ingenious but impractical. However, Dr. McCarroll was one of those people who would not take no for an answer, so she took her idea to the local women's club. The vote was unanimous in support of the project. Nevertheless, as the saying goes, some minds are like concrete—all mixed up and permanently set. She continued to face bureaucratic stubbornness for seven long years before her idea was implemented.

C. N. Hamilton was a staunch local supporter of Dr. McCarroll's concept, and when he became a member of the California Highway Commission in 1924, he convinced the commission to approve the painting of a five-mile-long experimental center line on Route 99. An additional test strip was also painted. Accidents on both stretches diminished dramatically, and soon the entire state boasted McCarroll lines on its highways. Most of the world has since followed suit.

Message: When you conceive an idea in which you fervently believe, go after that idea, especially if people you respect believe it's a good one. Hang in there because polite, pleasant persistence is often the key to accomplishment.

*An optimist is a fellow who believes a*
*housefly is looking for a way to get out.*

GEORGE JEAN NATHAN

# BE KIND AND LISTEN

Temper is far too valuable to lose, so watch yours
carefully and you probably won't lose it.

A wise person said that it's nice to be important, but it's
more important to be nice. Another "oldie" is that when
you're talking, you're not learning; it's only when you listen
that you learn.

Listening will help you avoid some embarrassments and
might even make you money. For example, when Tommy
Bolt was on the golf tour, he established a well-deserved
reputation for his temper. His breaking and throwing of
clubs became locker room fodder and a topic for media discussion. Once, in a tournament, he drew a caddie who had
a reputation for being a talker, so Bolt told him to keep quiet
and restrict his conversation to "Yes, Mr. Bolt" or "No, Mr.
Bolt."

As luck would have it, one of Bolt's shots stopped close
to a tree. To reach the green, he had to hit the ball under

a branch and over a lake. He carefully analyzed the situation and made a decision. However, as it frequently happens, halfway talking to his caddie and halfway talking to himself, he asked, "Should I hit it with my five iron?" The caddie, having been duly warned, responded, "No, Mr. Bolt." Bolt's temper and pride prompted him to say, "What do you mean, not a five iron? Just watch this shot!" The caddie, still following instructions, said, "No, Mr. Bolt!" Bolt wasn't listening. He took dead aim and hit the shot beautifully to the green. It stopped a couple of feet from the hole. With a look of self-satisfaction, Bolt handed the caddie his five iron and commented, "What do you think about that? And it's okay for you to talk now." "Mr. Bolt, that wasn't your ball," the caddie responded.

Hitting the wrong ball cost Tommy Bolt a two-shot penalty and lots of money. Message: be nice to people, especially those who serve you, and listen to what they have to say.

*Some of us learn from other people's mistakes,*
*and the rest of us have to be other people.*

# THE "SEAT" OF YOUR ATTITUDE

*Admitting a mistake is a beginning; correcting it is
a step forward; following through is success.*

Over the years I have spoken at several thousand functions
of virtually every description. I have spoken to groups of
twelve and once to a throng of sixty thousand. I have consistently noted one tendency in all audiences, especially in
sales organizations and leadership/management conferences.
Almost without exception the top salespeople are seated at
or very close to the front, depending on their vision and the
angle of the seats they have chosen.

Those people who already "know it all" or feel that they
do, or those people who consider this a waste of their time
or think they've "heard it all before," will invariably arrive
late or at the last moment, unprepared. They are also the
ones most likely to squirm in their seats, leave early, or talk
to the person next to them.

I've also observed that when these same people go to an

athletic or entertainment event, they want the best seat in the house. They generally arrive in plenty of time and are irritated when there are distractions from anyone else.

All of this is to say that front-row people by and large come to educational or inspirational meetings with great expectations. They come prepared to learn and take good notes. A study at Harvard University revealed that people who get the most out of meetings (a) come with the expectation of getting great ideas, (b) take good notes, and (c) talk with colleagues about what they learned and compare notes. This way they reinforce what they learned and pick up points they missed from the other person. In short, these people are winners because they plan to win, prepare to win, and expect to win. That's a good approach to life.

*You can't be a smart cookie if you*
*have a crummy attitude.*

JOHN MAXWELL

# CONCENTRATE ON YOUR RESPONSIBILITIES

We cannot become what we need to be
by remaining what we are.

From time to time I have the privilege of speaking to university and professional football teams. On other occasions, I have an opportunity to speak to coaches at local high school and college levels. On one of these occasions, I heard former University of Texas coach John Mackovic make an interesting observation that I believe is applicable to any field of endeavor.

He said that when his team was on the offense, he was "interested" in the defensive alignment, but was "vitally concerned" about what his players were going to do. He observed that if he had recruited the right players, coached and trained them properly, and if he and his coaches had developed a good game plan, he was confident that his team was going to score more points than the opposition.

He then reversed the observation, assuming the opposition had the ball. He was interested in what their athletes and their game plan called for, but he was "vitally concerned" about his defensive alignment and what his players were going to do.

That lesson can be applied regardless of what we do. Be interested in what others are doing, but be vitally concerned about your own performance. If coworkers are late and slack in their performance, view that as an opportunity to make a bigger contribution and climb the corporate ladder even faster.

Remember, if you're in a leadership position, your responsibility is to choose the right people, then train and inspire them to use their ability. Peter Drucker said it well: "Leadership is lifting a person's vision to higher sights, the raising of a person's performance to a higher standard, the building of a personality beyond its normal limitations." Buy that concept and your leadership effectiveness and the performance of your people will improve substantially.

*Boss, as he fires an employee: "Look on the bright side.*
*You always said you wanted to be an entrepreneur."*

# SUCCESS IS A PARTNERSHIP

*A lot of people have gone further than they thought they could because someone else thought they could.*

A cliché declares that behind every successful man there is a surprised mother-in-law. In most, if not all, cases, success is a direct result of the efforts of the individual and the support and encouragement of another person or persons.

Like the fellow says, when you see a turtle on a fence post, you can rest assured that it did not get there by itself. When you see an individual climbing the success ladder and reaching the top, you know they did not get there entirely as a result of their own efforts. In virtually every case, the person had hope and encouragement from others.

Nathaniel Hawthorne is a good example. He was discouraged and had a broken heart when he went home to tell his wife, Sophia, that he was a failure because he had been fired from his job in the customhouse. Upon hearing the news, she startled him with an exuberant exclamation of joy. "Now," she said triumphantly, "you can write your book!" To that, Hawthorne responded with the question, "What are we going to live on while I am writing this book?" To his surprise and delight, she opened a drawer and drew out a substantial sum of money. "Where did you get that?" he asked. "I've always known you were a man of genius," she told him, "and I knew that someday you would write a masterpiece, so every week, out of the money you gave me for housekeeping, I saved part of it. Here's enough to last us for a whole year." From his wife's trust, confidence, thrift, and careful planning came one of the classics of American literature—*The Scarlet Letter*. That story of one person supporting another can be repeated a few thousand times—or make that a few million. It happens all the time.

If that is your story in life, I hope you're careful to give credit to those who assisted you.

*Put all our congressmen together and they weigh about 96,000 pounds. It's hard to get anything that weighs 48 tons to move quickly.*

CHARLIE "TREMENDOUS" JONES

# LOOKING FOR MUTUALLY
# BENEFICIAL SOLUTIONS

A winner is big enough to admit his mistakes, smart enough
to profit from them, and strong enough to correct them.

JOHN MAXWELL

Every problem has a solution, but the best solutions are
always mutually beneficial. Howard Putnam, in his book
*The Winds of Turbulence*, tells this story. Baylor Hospital
in Dallas had a major problem. They could not get enough
nurses who were willing to work weekends, because they
wanted to be with their families. But the leadership recognized that there were also a number of nurses, particularly
those who had young children, who wanted to be with their
children during the week so they could spend as much time
with them as possible. In most cases, married nurses had
husbands who worked a Monday-through-Friday schedule.
Single mothers had an even greater need to be with their

children as much as possible, so the thinking was very simple: *Can we meet the needs of* all *these nurses?*

Leadership then asked the question, How can we help these mothers get what they want? How can we help the full-time nurses get what they want? The solution, as Mr. Putnam points out, was so obvious, one wonders why it took them so long to come up with the answer. Here's what they did: Since weekend work is generally considered overtime, they decided to make Saturday and Sunday twelve-hour shifts, for a total of twenty-four hours of duty. They paid these nurses for a full forty-hour week, so those nurses were elated. On the other hand, the nurses who simply did not want to work overtime or weekends were elated that they could maintain their normal schedule. This truly was a win-win situation. The weekend nurses won, the full-time nurses won, and the hospital and patients were also big winners.

That's leadership at its best. The message is clear: examine your alternatives, explore what the problem might be, and ask yourself the question, *Is the solution in the problem?* In many cases it is.

*My problem is that I'm always good*
*when nobody is watching.*

DENNIS THE MENACE

# LITTLE THINGS DO MAKE BIG DIFFERENCES

Open your eyes and you will undoubtedly see a hundred
things you can and should express gratitude for. Do it.

If my watch is four minutes slow and I show up for a noon
flight at 12:04 p.m., you know what will happen. I have an
arrangement with the airlines that if I'm not there when my
flight is scheduled to leave, they are to go ahead and leave
without me. They have always lived up to their end of the
agreement.

Somebody once said that honesty in little things is no
little thing. Also, the smallest good deed is better than the
grandest intention. How right these statements are. On the
serious side, a little thing can be enormously significant.
Retired Brigadier General Robinson Risner was a prisoner
of war in North Vietnam for more than seven years. He was
in solitary confinement for five of those years. He suffered
from cold, heat, malnutrition, and lack of fresh air. He was
totally deprived of any human comfort. He jogged in his

cell by the hour. When he became so frustrated he had to scream, he stuffed his underwear into his mouth to muffle the scream. He would not give his captors the satisfaction of knowing his frustration.

One day, in the depths of despair, General Risner lay down on the floor and looked all around his small rectangular-shaped cell. He put his eye next to the cinder blocks, hoping that there would be a crack in one of them. Fortunately, there was a minute opening and he saw single leaf. Later he stated that seeing that evidence of life outside was a tremendously uplifting and life-changing event.

When I heard his story, most of my complaints in life suddenly fell into context, and I resolved to be more appreciative of the many blessings I had instead of complaining about what I did not have. Fact: a quiet glance around you will reveal many blessings that you have already received and will continue to receive. Expressing appreciation for these blessings is a winning approach to life.

Diner: "I can't eat this soup." Waiter: "Sorry, sir, I'll call the manager." Diner: "Mr. Manager, I can't eat this soup." Manager: "I'll call the chef." Diner: "Mr. Chef, I can't eat this soup." Chef: "What's wrong with it?" Diner: "Nothing. I haven't got a spoon."

# LEADERSHIP THAT LEADS

Before you can lead anyone else, you must
first learn to manage yourself.

Danny Cox's book *Leadership When the Heat's On* offers exciting and valuable tips on leadership. Here are just a few of them:

First, employees get better as their manager does, and they really don't care how smart or talented you are. What people care about is your attitude toward them.

Second, leaders have contagious enthusiasm, and as Cox points out, if you don't have that enthusiasm, please understand that whatever you do have is also contagious.

Third, when you make a list of things to do for the next day, do not go to number two as you finish the first one. Instead, understand that what was number two now becomes number one, and physiologically, that task becomes more important when you give it a higher priority. Follow that procedure through numbers two, three, and so on.

Danny Cox also lists the ten ingredients in his recipe for leadership: (1) high ethics, (2) high energy, (3) hard work, (4) enthusiasm, (5) goal-orientation, (6) courage, (7) focus on priorities, (8) nonconformity, (9) levelheadedness, and (10) commitment to developing employees.

In an interview with George Foreman, Cox said he noticed George's nose and decided that here was a guy who understood pain, so he asked him, "How did you stand all that pain to become the heavyweight champ?" George answered, "If I see what I want real good in my mind, I don't notice any pain in getting it." Cox then points out that idea holds true for all of us.

Danny Cox has given us some excellent advice. I believe if more of us will take it, we'll produce more leaders in this country. Listen to Danny Cox.

*Many senior art workshop participants were trying their hand at various skills for the first time. From behind the partition separating my oil painting class from the watercolor class came these words of sweet revenge: "I think I'll send these to my grandchildren to hang on their refrigerator."*

CONTRIBUTED TO *READER'S DIGEST* BY LYNDA ALONGI

# HE GOT BETTER, NOT BITTER

*When (not if) troubles and problems come your way, remember that the only way to the mountaintop is through the valley.*

One of my favorite people, and certainly one of America's finest communicators, was Neal Jeffrey. Neal, as quarterback, led the Baylor Bears football team to the Southwest Conference Championship in 1974, and then went on to play in the NFL for San Diego. He later addressed many youth groups as well as adult businesspeople. He was truly one of the most humorous, sincere, and capable speakers I ever heard. The interesting thing was that Neal was a stutterer. However, he had chosen to make stuttering an asset, not a problem.

Now think about what you just read. Someone who was both a very successful quarterback and a public speaker who stuttered doesn't compute in the minds of most people. Neal Jeffrey took a negative and turned it into a positive. After beginning his speeches, he told audiences that in case they hadn't noticed, he stuttered. Then with a big smile, he'd say, "Sometimes I do get hung up a little bit. But don't worry. I guarantee you something's coming!" The audience invariably responded enthusiastically.

Neal was the classic example of an outstanding individual who chose to make an obstacle an asset. The obstacle forced him to be more creative and to do more reading, research, and studying so he could most effectively turn that liability into an asset. As a result he got better, not bitter. He was better, not in spite of his stutter, but because of his stutter. Neal reached goal after goal in all areas of his life. I believe that you can do the same thing.

All of us have liabilities that can hold us back or propel us forward. In most cases, the choice is ours. So take your obstacles or liabilities, recognize and evaluate them, and then find a way to turn them into assets.

*Teacher: "Greg, tell the class what is meant by compromise." Greg: "A compromise is a deal in which two people get what neither of them wanted."*

# IT'S BETTER TO GIVE

Truly successful people in life are givers and forgivers.

"When Wally Jansen told me about my company's Christmas 'trip to the island' tradition," says Phillip Kelly, "I was intrigued. Ten days before Christmas the two hundred Puerto Rican families in this particular parish would gather, and each family would place five dollars in the pot, which was about a day's pay for a fruit picker back then. Each family would write its name on a slip of paper. Then they would blindfold someone to draw the name of the family that would get to go home for Christmas—two glorious weeks on the island, and enough money to buy Christmas presents for everyone. I went to the drawing that year, my first Christmas with the community, but it was going to be Wally Jansen's last. Wally was retiring after working forty years with the company, and for the last twenty-five he had been the canning factory foreman.

"By three o'clock everyone had parted with their five

dollars and the announcer called the committee onstage to witness the drawing. Then they called me up to draw the name of the lucky family. On went the blindfold and I was led to the drum. I reached in, sorted out a handful, and finally settled on one. I opened the slip of paper and read, 'Wally Jansen.' The cheers were deafening. Everyone surrounded him, hugging him, crying, congratulating him, wishing him a merry Christmas and a joyous trip. While the commotion continued, I casually reached back into the drum and drew out a handful of slips and opened a couple. Each one, in different writing, carried the same name— Wally Jansen."

I imagine that the Wally Jansen family was thrilled beyond words, but I believe the joy that each person felt, thinking that maybe he or she had written the name "Wally Jansen" that was drawn, was greater still. Think about that. Become a giver, and you will be happier on your trip to the top.

*My doctor gave me six months to live. When I told him*
*I couldn't pay the bill, he gave me six more months.*

HENNY YOUNGMAN

# WE'RE BOTH ON THE SAME SIDE

Remember that when you're standing on the edge of a
cliff, the best way to make progress is to back up.

One of my favorite stories concerns a young lad who was
confronted by three bullies with violence in mind.

Quickly, the little guy drew a line on the ground, stepped
back several feet, looked the biggest bully in the eye, and
said, "Now, you just step over that line." Confidently, the
big bully stepped over the line, preparing to commit may-
hem on the little guy. Quickly the little fellow grinned and
said, "Now we're both on the same side."

Physically, they were both on the same side. But emo-
tionally they were still some distance apart. The smaller boy
improved his chances of getting on the same side emotion-
ally by his touch of wit and wisdom. This is an excellent
combination to defuse most crisis situations and represents
a major step in solving whatever problems exist.

There are several lessons parents, managers, and

educators can learn from this little vignette. First, whether it is a parent-child, management-labor, or teacher-student situation, both people really are on the same side and the best way for either side to win is for both sides to win. Second, a sense of humor can be very helpful in removing communication barriers by revealing your human side and establishing rapport. Third, sometimes it's necessary for the big bully (the person in authority) to move to the other side of the table (across the line). This lets associates, children, or employees clearly understand that they really are on the same side and the authority is open to listening to ideas from both sides of that line. The fourth message is that it is always important and to our advantage to maintain our perspective by being open and fair-minded as we look at life from the other person's perspective.

*Enjoy your kids while they're young and still on your side.*

# REWARD YOURSELF

*Speaking of "mere words" is like speaking of "mere dynamite."*

The late William Arthur Ward was and is one of my favorite writers. His insights and ability to put a philosophy of life into a few words were truly remarkable. Here is a sample from his book *Reward Yourself*:

> A man phoned his physician and excitedly explained: "Please come at once, Doctor. My son has swallowed my fountain pen."
>
> The doctor replied, "I'll be right over. But what are you doing in the meanwhile?"
>
> "Using a pencil," answered the father.
>
> What we do "in the meanwhile" is of vital importance to our lives—and to the lives of others. What we do with our leisure time can build our character or destroy it. It came make our fortune or mar it.
>
> While we wait for a traffic light to change, we can pray for our president, our nation, and the world.

While we wait for an elevator we can be still and know that God is, and that He is still in charge of the universe.

While we drive or ride to work, we can affirmatively and joyously meditate on that which is true, pure, lovely, and positive.

While we wash dishes, mow the lawn, or perform other tasks that require less than our complete attention, we can sing, whistle, or hum the tunes of great songs and hymns that inevitably make life more beautiful for us and for our fellow human beings.

While we sit in the waiting room of our physician or dentist, we can thank God for dedicated professional people, and we can pray for those patients who might be anxious, fearful, despondent, or in pain.

What we do with our golden "in the meanwhile" moments can enrich and inspire, encourage and uplift, bless and brighten our important corner of the world.

These are more than words on a piece of paper—they present a philosophy of life. Adopt it for your own, and you truly will reward yourself.

*Man to friend: "I figured out why inflation is still here. Everybody's earning money five days a week, but the government is spending it seven days a week."*

DON REBER IN THE READING, PENNSYLVANIA, *TIMES*

# PERSISTENCE REALLY DOES PAY

Perseverance is very important to success. How else would two snails have made it to the ark?

For eight years the struggling young writer wrote incredible numbers of short stories and articles for publication, and for eight long years they were rejected. Fortunately, he didn't give up, and for that he—and America—will always be grateful.

He spent much of his time in the navy writing a mountain of routine reports and letters. He learned how to say things eloquently, yet concisely. After his stint in the navy, he tried desperately hard to make it as a writer, but despite those eight years and hundreds of stories and articles, he was unable to sell even one. On one occasion, however, an editor wrote an encouraging note on the rejection slip. It simply said, "Nice try."

I think you'll agree that most of us would not rate that little comment very high on the encouragement list, but it literally brought tears to the young writer's eyes. He was given new hope and continued to persist. He simply would not give up. Finally, after many years of effort, he wrote a book that has deeply affected the entire world and helped him to become one of the most influential writers of the '70s. I'm speaking of Alex Haley and his book *Roots*, which was made into one of the most-watched television miniseries of all time.

The message is clear: if you have a dream and if you really believe you have some ability that can be expressed, pursue that dream; don't give up. Hang in there! Who knows? Maybe on your next effort somebody will say, "Nice try." That might be all the encouragement you'll need. Remember, success might be just around the corner, over the next hill, or at the end of that next effort.

*I'm way overdue for a promotion. I've made*
*so many lateral moves I'm beside myself.*

GARY APPLE

# I'M C2 AND FAT-FREE

*Remember, happiness doesn't depend upon who you are
or what you have. It depends solely on what you think.*

DALE CARNEGIE

Several years ago I heard about a fellow who returned a
phone call, and when the phone was answered, the response
was "286-7495." The gentleman replied, "Yes, I'm returning
Mr. Anderson's call," and the operator said, "Who is this?"
He responded, "233-9191."

It seems to be true that many people have become mere
numbers in our uncaring, technological world. This was
brought home to me recently when I checked in at the gate
for one of my numerous flights. When I showed my ticket
with the boarding pass to the gate agent, he picked up his
microphone and said to the flight attendant aboard, "C2 is
here." What he meant was simply that I had seat C2 and was
at the gate. I kind of laughed and said to the fellow, "Well,

that's the first time I've been identified as a seat number." He smiled as I walked aboard the airplane, and sat down, and we took off. When mealtime came, the flight attendant began listing the menu choices for the passengers. When he got to me, I said, "I believe I have a special meal." He turned to another attendant and said, "Fat-free is here." Since I prefer to be called Zig, I'm glad the names C2 and Fat-Free did not stick.

I find it amusing and yet, in a strange way, a little sad that we've reached that point in life when we can so casually deal with one another as a number or a letter. That's especially true at this time in our history when mergers, downsizing, rightsizing, buyouts, early retirement, and bankruptcy have created stress and fear in the marketplace. Today people need hope and encouragement, combined with genuine care and concern from those with whom we deal on a regular basis. When we pay our bills with a check or credit card, we like to be called by name. I'm not C2 and Fat-Free; I'm a human being—and so are you. Let's treat each other that way.

*Understand that anybody who is*
*somebody to anybody is somebody.*

# THE PART-TIMER MADE IT BIG-TIME

Success is determined not by what you get for reaching
your destination, but by what you become by reaching it.

When Dean Sanders was a college student, he went to work part time with Sam's Wholesale Warehouse. Later he became president of the multimillion-dollar company. I met and came to know Dean when I was speaking for Sam's grand opening of new stores.

One morning it was my pleasure to address Sam's staff at a breakfast before they opened for business. Dean's openness with his staff, his "shirtsleeve" approach, and his friendliness were refreshing, but I was really impressed when I noticed that Dean was moving some empty plates and cups to the trash barrel. As I observed him, I wondered how many presidents of multimillion-dollar corporations would be doing such a thing. First, would they be at a working breakfast; second, would they mingle so easily and freely with the staff—which included highly paid executives and hourly wage earners—and third, would they be cleaning up the breakfast dishes when so many other people were around?

The thing that struck me is that Dean did it so matter-of-factly without giving it any obvious thought or the feeling, "Well, somebody's gotta do this and nobody else is doing it, so I suppose I will." It was an attitude of, if it was there, it needed doing; he was the closest and therefore the most logical one to do it.

It's true: "He who is greatest among you shall be your servant" (Matthew 23:11 NKJV). Today many people think others should serve them, but the reality is that those who serve best are those who will lead the most. Think about it. Adopt the servant's attitude (without being servile).

*Columnist Ray Ratto in the San Francisco Examiner on a potential problem facing the 49ers one season: "Carmen Policy is a lawyer. Steve Young is a lawyer. Center Bart Oates is a lawyer. Marc Trestman, the 49ers' new offensive coordinator, is a lawyer. God help us all if they ever disagree on third and eight."*

# CONVICTION IS THE KEY

A person is persuaded more by the depth of your
convictions than by the breadth of your knowledge.

The late Mary Crowley frequently commented that one person with a conviction would do more than a hundred who had only an interest. Commitment is the key to staying the course and completing the project. Conviction always precedes commitment.

When you're convinced as a salesperson that you are selling a marvelous product, your demeanor, body language, voice inflection, and facial expressions communicate to the prospect that you fervently believe you're offering something of value. Many times the prospect will buy, not because of their belief in the product, goods, or service, but because of the belief of the salesperson in the product being offered.

Our feelings are transferable. Courage can be and frequently is transferred to another person. Convictions are the same. The teacher who fervently believes in the message they deliver will persuade the student by the very depth of that conviction. One of my favorite Mary Kay Ash quotes is "Many people have gone a lot farther than they thought they could because someone else thought they could." In short, their confidence, born of someone else's conviction, had enabled them to make it. Conviction comes from knowledge and a feeling that what we're teaching, doing, or selling is absolutely right. When we transfer that conviction to those within our spheres of influence, they and society benefit.

Show me a person with deep convictions, and I'll show you a person who has made a commitment to deliver those convictions to others. Show me a great leader, and I'll show you a person of deep convictions who is able to attract followers because of those convictions. I'll also show you a person who is happy in what they are doing and far more successful than people who do not have those convictions. Message: buy that idea, develop those convictions, and make that commitment.

*I'm certain all of us have heard about the employee who always gives his company an honest day's work. Of course, it takes him a week to do it.*

EXECUTIVE SPEECHWRITER NEWSLETTER

# A STRANGE WAY TO SHOW LOVE

It is not necessary that we should all think
exactly alike, but we should all think.

The giraffe is the largest mammal that gives birth to its young while standing up. I don't speak "giraffe," but I can imagine what the baby giraffe must be thinking when he bounces on the ground from that great height. He just left warm, cushioned quarters in which all his needs, comforts, and security were provided. Now he finds himself bouncing off (comparatively speaking) hard, cold, unwelcoming ground.

Almost immediately thereafter, a new trauma occurs in the baby giraffe's life. As he struggles to his knees, Mama Giraffe gets busy "persuading" him to stand up. She does this as he wobbles to his feet by giving him a swift kick to prod him to faster action. No sooner does he reach his feet than Mama delivers a booming kick that knocks the baby giraffe back down.

Again, I don't speak "giraffe," but I can well imagine the baby giraffe thinking, *Well, make up your mind, Mom! First you kicked me to make me stand up. Then you kicked me back down!* Interestingly enough, once the baby giraffe is back on the ground, Mama Giraffe again starts kicking and nudging until he stands back up. That process is repeated several times because Mama Giraffe loves her baby. Or is it instinct?

Who can say with certainty? However, this we know for certain: Baby Giraffe is a prime delicacy for carnivorous animals, which are a part of his environment. Mama Giraffe knows that the only chance of survival for her baby is to be able to quickly get up and move out of harm's way. Yes, kicking the baby up and down seems like a strange way to show love. But for a baby giraffe it is the ultimate expression of love. Caution: that approach definitely won't work in the "people" world, but the principle will. Real love is evidenced when you do what is best for the other person, whether or not they appreciate it at that moment.

*They say it can't be done, but sometimes*
*that doesn't always work.*

BASEBALL LEGEND CASEY STENGEL

# ONE INCIDENT CAN CHANGE US FOREVER

Our purpose in life should be to see one another
through, not through one another.

In the later 1800s, a rich boy and a poor boy lived in the same neighborhood. The rich boy wore nice clothes, lived in a nice house, and had plenty of good, nutritious food to eat. The poor boy lived in a cheap house, wore ragged clothes, and did not have much of anything to eat. One day the boys got into a scuffle. In the struggle the rich boy won. The poor boy got up, dusted himself off, and told the rich kid that if he had the proper food to eat as the rich boy did, he would have won. Then the poor boy turned and walked away. The rich kid just stood there. He was numbed by what the poor boy said. His heart was broken because he knew that it was true.

The rich boy never forgot that experience. From that day on he revolted against any favored treatment because he was rich. He made it a point to wear inexpensive clothing;

he intentionally endured the hardships faced by people who were poor. His family was often embarrassed by the way he dressed, but despite family pressure, the young boy never again took advantage of his wealth.

History omits the name of the poor boy, but the rich boy who developed such compassion for poor people made them his life's work. His name is recorded in history. He dedicated his life to service and became a world-class physician, serving in Africa. His name was Albert Schweitzer.

I'm not suggesting that we all be as selfless as Albert Schweitzer, but I do believe that we need to be more in tune with the thinking and feelings of others. Very few people have had as much impact on the world as Albert Schweitzer did. Even fewer people have gotten as much satisfaction out of life as he did.

*As optimist is a person who will use his*
*last dollar to buy a money belt.*

# LEADERS ACCEPT RESPONSIBILITY

*The real reward for a thing well done is to have done it.*

Hakeem Olajuwon was the all-pro center for the Houston Rockets, the world champions of the National Basketball Association in 1994 and 1995. The year before the Rockets won their first championship against the New York Knicks, Hakeem realized that because he was the team leader, his responsibility was more pronounced than anyone else's. He recognized that he had a weakness in his game, which was the fifteen-foot jump shot. Think about it. He earned a multimillion-dollar income and had been all-pro for six consecutive years. However, he felt that the team would never win a championship until he improved his shooting from fifteen feet.

Before the 1993–94 season, he went to the gym every day and practiced five hundred fifteen-foot jump shots. That's an incredible test of building strength, endurance, and improvement in performance. In 1994, when the Houston Rockets defeated the New York Knicks in seven games, there was only one game with more than a five-point difference in the score. Replays revealed that had Hakeem not improved his shooting percentage from fifteen feet, the New York Knicks would have won instead of the Houston Rockets.

Here are some questions for you to think about: First, do you believe that Hakeem was popular with his teammates as a result of the extra effort he made to help bring the championship to Houston? Second, do you believe Hakeem was thrilled to win that world championship ring? And third, do you understand why he got a significant raise when his contract was up for renewal?

It's true, you can have everything in life you want if you will just help enough other people get what they want. Hakeem helped his teammates, the owners, and the fans gain that championship. He was big-time because he, too, was part of the championship team and, as a matter of fact, was named the most valuable player for his tremendous efforts.

*If you are wearing out the seat of your pants*
*before you do your shoe soles, you're making*
*too many contacts in the wrong place.*

# THE YOUNG PERSUADER

The best gifts are wrapped in love and tied with heartstrings.

A few days after my second daughter was born, I had to take a trip to South Carolina from our Knoxville, Tennessee, home. On the way back, a sudden snowstorm left me and a few hundred other motorists stranded for the night. Fortunately, I was stranded directly behind a nice, warm Greyhound bus. The driver was kind enough to permit me to climb aboard and spend the night. The next morning the highways were cleared and I drove on home.

I had no sooner pulled into the driveway and gotten inside the house than my wife said we needed more baby supplies. I slipped my heavy coat back on and was headed for the door when my soon-to-be four-year-old daughter, Suzan, said, "Daddy, take me with you." I explained to her that the weather was bad, I would be gone only a few minutes, and it would be best for her to stay home. As only a four-year-old can, she said, "But, Daddy, I will be so lonely."

I said, "Now, Doll, your mother is here and so is your new baby sister, and Lizzie (who was our live-in nanny)." Then she looked at me and said, "But, Daddy, I'll be lonely for you." I don't need to tell you that she went with me to the store that day.

In retrospect, that is persuasion at its absolute best—straight from the heart, without guile or any subterfuge. In a direct, simple way Suzan made me feel important—I was the one she was going to be lonely for. I believe that if we play it straight, speak from the heart, and be open and direct with people in a loving way, we improve our communication skills dramatically and our persuasiveness goes up.

*No person ever ended his eyesight by looking on the bright side.*

# THOSE EXCUSES WE MAKE

You're not finished when you are defeated;
you are finished when you quit.

My brother, the late Judge Ziglar, loved to tell the story of the fellow who went next door to borrow his neighbor's lawn mower. The neighbor explained that he could not let him use the lawn mower because all the flights had been canceled from New York to Los Angeles. The borrower asked him what canceled flights from New York to Los Angeles had to do with borrowing his lawn mower. "It doesn't have anything to do with it, but if I don't want to let you use my lawn mower, one excuse is as good as another."

The neighbor was absolutely right. One excuse is as good as another because an excuse, in most cases, is nothing but a denial or refusal to accept responsibility. My trusty 1828 *Webster's Dictionary of the English Language* says to *excuse* is "to justify" or "to vindicate," "a plea offered in extenuation of a fault or irregular deportment." George

Washington Carver said that 99 percent of failures come from people who have a habit of making excuses. Harold Sherman said, "It's mighty soothing to the ego to be able to alibi our failures. I've done it, you've done it, and it has seemed to help temporarily. But the alibis have proved costly in the long run, because they've kept us from facing the truth about ourselves. They have kept us from going to work and correcting our mistakes, eliminating our weaknesses, developing our talents, improving our character." And finally, "Don't make excuses, make good."

These little gems are invaluable and should force each of us to think. When we do that, we won't make excuses—we will make good.

*There are approximately two hundred thousand useless words in the English language—and many politicians repeatedly use most of them.*

# TRUTH IS STRANGER AND MORE EXCITING THAN FICTION

Good news—you can change. Make sure it's for the better.

*Gone with the Wind* is a classic novel. *Scarlett* is the follow-up book to this classic. However, the original story had more than just a kernel of truth in it. There was a Rhett Butler, but his real name was Rhett Turnipseed. Scarlett O'Hara was Emelyn Louise Hannon. Yes, Rhett did walk out on her and join the Confederate army. When the war was over, Rhett Turnipseed became a drifter and gambler. He ended up in Nashville, where his life was turned around on Easter morning in 1871, when he attended a Methodist revival meeting and became a committed Christian.

Soon after, Rhett enrolled at Vanderbilt University and became a Methodist preacher. Reverend Rhett was worried about a young woman in his flock who had run away and was working in a house of prostitution in St. Louis. Rhett rode off to look for her and found her. Incredibly enough, the madam was his former love, Emelyn Louise Hannon—or Scarlett. She refused to let Rhett see the young woman, so Rhett challenged her to a game of cards. If he won, the young girl would be free; if Scarlett won, she would remain. Rhett won.

Fortunately, the story ends well for everyone. The young girl married well and became the matriarch of a leading family in the state. Later, Emelyn, so impressed with the change in Rhett's life, also became a Christian and joined the Methodist church. Eventually, she opened an orphanage for Cherokee children. She died in 1903. Her grave is marked to this day.

The message is twofold. First, truth really is stranger than fiction; and second, yes, people can change. Going from gambler to preacher and from madam to operator of an orphanage for displaced children represents quite a change. So don't give up. You can change.

*Comic J. Scott Homan said he's been trying to*
*get into shape doing twenty sit-ups each morning.*
*That may not sound like a lot, but you can*
*only hit the snooze button so many times.*

# THE ULTIMATE OPTIMIST

Personality has the power to open doors, but
it takes character to keep them open.

Most people consider me an optimist because I laughingly
state that I would take my last dollar and buy a money belt.
I'd even go after Moby Dick in a rowboat and take the tar-
tar sauce with me! However, I've got to confess that I don't
hold a candle to the ultimate lady optimist who lived in a
retirement home. One day, a distinguished-looking gentleman also became a resident. As luck would have it, the first
day they sat across the table from each other at lunch. After
a few minutes he grew uncomfortable because she was staring intently at him. He finally expressed his discomfort and
queried her as to why she was staring. She responded that
she was staring because he reminded her so much of her
third husband—same demeanor, same smile, same height,
weight—everything. The gentleman replied in some shock,

"Third husband! How many times have you been married?" The lady smilingly said, "Twice." Yup. That's optimism!

I've got to confess I'm a pragmatic optimist myself. I love the story of the gentleman who was being given a tour of the Mann Auditorium in Tel Aviv. The tour guide was pointing out the features of the incredible structure. The stonework was unbelievably beautiful. The wall tapestries, paintings, and gold inlays were absolutely gorgeous. Finally, the tourist said, "I assume you named the facility for Horace Mann, the famous author." The tour guide answered with a smile, "No, we named it after Fredric Mann from Philadelphia." The tourist remarked, "Fredric Mann? What did he write?" The tour guide said, "A check." Now, that's being pragmatic!

It might interest you to know that the 1828 *Webster's Dictionary* identifies the optimist in complimentary terms, but says nothing about the pessimist. The word *pessimist* was not in our vocabulary at that time. It's a modern invention that I believe we should "dis-invent." I encourage you to become an optimist—a pragmatic one, that is.

*The time to make friends is before you need them.*

ETHEL BARRYMORE

# DO SOMETHING NICE TODAY

You cannot live a perfect day without doing something
for someone who will never be able to repay you.

JOHN WOODEN

America is getting older. Social Security faces a crisis. Many
people are wondering what they can do when their work
life ends. Neva Marie Mabbott once offered some heart-
warming thoughts:

"When surgery loomed on my personal horizon, one
of my concerns was financial. As a widow living on Social
Security and with what I made working three hours a day in
a Montessori playground and nap room, I could ill afford to
take a month off for recuperation. Fortunately, that worry
was nipped in the bud by a call from another widow from
my church. 'Neva? This is Madeleine. I just called your
boss and made arrangements to keep you on the payroll in
December while I work in your place.' 'But I can't let you

do that,' I said. But Madeleine replied, 'Now, now, it's all arranged. I've done this kind of work in my home and I'll come in a couple of days before you go to the hospital to learn your routine. Besides, I want you to rest, not worry about a loss of income.'

"My thanks barely made it past the large lump in my throat. December brought rest, reading, and writing time. It was the most beautiful Advent and Christmas of my life. Madeleine is surely a wonderful example of a sacrificial giver."

There's nothing that will make you feel better than doing something for someone else. You might not be able to take a month off, but you could babysit for a young mother with errands to run but no money for a babysitter. You could spend an hour in a nursing home, loving, talking, and listening to those who are there. You could deliver a few "meals on wheels," or help at the Salvation Army as they serve the underprivileged.

*A perfect example of the power of prayer is when a blizzard closes the schools on the day of a big exam.*

DOUG LARSON

# THREE SIDES TO THE STORY

Your unhappiness is not due to your want of a fortune or high position or fame or sufficient vitamins. It is due not to a want of something outside of you, but to a want of something inside you. You were made for perfect happiness. No wonder everything short of God disappoints you.

FULTON J. SHEEN

My mother often said, "There are three sides to every story—your side, their side, and the right side."

Over the years, I have come to the conclusion that in most cases she was right. How often, when we hear the first account of a story, does it appear that someone is guilty without a doubt? Later we get the other side of the story and completely change our minds. "Don't rush to judgment" is good advice.

A typical example is something that took place at our company. An employee reported an incident to me in which he was not directly involved, but he had heard about it "through the grapevine." The evidence seemed compelling that a serious error in judgment by a key staff member had occurred. However, after talking with those directly involved, who had all the relevant information, the picture changed dramatically.

As it developed, there were three sides. Each was right, but critical information was incomplete. This led to the erroneous original conclusion that a serious error had been made. What was needed was that old Paul Harvey standby, "the rest of the story," which validated the fact that there were three sides.

I encourage you, particularly if you're in a management or decision-making position regarding other people, to carefully hear what the messenger is saying. Make no decisions, promises, or judgments until you have heard the other side of the story. Take that approach and you'll win more friends and influence more people.

*Most people who berate their luck never*
*think to question their judgment.*

# SHE PASSED THE TEST—CAN YOU?

It's okay to retire from a job, but you
should never retire from work.

Major surgery requires not only a skilled surgeon but a number of skilled assistants to make certain that everything happens as it should. They function as a team. No one person, regardless of how brilliant they are, could pull off a major operation alone.

Recently, in a major medical center, a new head nurse was starting her first assignment. She was in charge of all the nurses on the operating room team. She had full responsibility for performing all the duties nurses perform. When the surgery was complete, the surgeon said, "Okay, it's time to close the incision. I need the sutures." The new head nurse responded, "Doctor, you used twelve sponges; we've only removed eleven." The surgeon assured her that all the sponges had been removed and he was ready to suture. She replied, "Doctor, you used twelve sponges; only eleven have been removed." With a bit of irritation in his voice, the doctor said, "I will accept full responsibility." At that point, the nurse's temper flew and she apparently stomped her foot and said, "Doctor, think of the patient!" When she said that, the doctor smiled, lifted his foot, and revealed the twelfth sponge. He looked at the nurse and said, "You'll do." Her integrity had been tested; she passed with flying colors.

The question is this: How many of us, under identical circumstances, would have risked offending the surgeon, remembering that there was a possibility we had miscounted? But this nurse felt the patient's life and health were at stake, and she, without hesitation, did the right thing. Over the long haul, that's the best way to get to the top and stay there.

*Team-builders are the tea bags of life. They
perform when the water is hot.*

ROGER STAUBACH

# DAD, YOU *DO* CHOOSE YOUR DAUGHTER'S HUSBAND

If what you believe doesn't affect how you
live, then it isn't very important.

DICK NOGLEBERG

Don't misunderstand. I'm not suggesting that you go through the computer or the neighborhood selecting the husband you believe would be appropriate for your daughter. But I would like to point out that you *do* help your daughter select her future husband. The process starts when your little girl is happily sitting on your knee or riding on your back. The truth is, the first knowledge our daughters acquire about relationships with the opposite sex comes from their fathers. What you teach your daughter about how men treat women becomes the cornerstone of her expectations. If you treat your wife with courtesy and respect, your daughter will file that in her memory bank as the way she should be treated by her future husband.

When your daughter sees you loving her mother and treating her with respect, she comes to know that men should treat their wives that way. However, if your daughter sees you abuse her mother, she learns that's the way men treat women and so she's not surprised—though she obviously doesn't like it—if her husband abuses her. This is especially true if it happens in small steps during the courtship process and gradually gets worse once she is married.

When I married Shelley, one of the things my wife's mother told her was "You've made a lifetime deal, but if he ever abuses you, you've got a home you can come to." By the strangest of coincidences, that's what we told our children. This communication to one of our daughters possibly helped her—and us—avoid a tragic mistake.

So, Dad, all this really says is that if you love your little girl, you will treat her and her mother with respect and dignity. If you do, chances are excellent your daughter will choose her husband wisely. In fact, he will probably be just like the guy old Dad would have chosen.

*Vanity—People should not forget the mama whale's advice to her baby: "Remember, it is only when you spout off that you get harpooned."*

# THAT FIRST IMPRESSION

*He who gains a victory over other men is strong, but
he who gains a victory over himself is all-powerful.*

LAO-TZU

It's true that you have one chance to make a first impression. Despite this fact, American business is rife with receptionists who are not pleasant, courteous, upbeat, or even understandable. Many companies apparently feel that anybody can answer the telephone. While it is true that anyone can be taught the mechanics of answering the telephone, lasting impressions are made—especially on first-time callers—of the type of company you have by the way that phone is answered.

We once received an exciting letter from one of our suppliers. The gentleman was the director of sales for his corporation. He commented with considerable enthusiasm that when he phoned our company, he first got Lou, and then on the second call, Barbara answered. His verbatim comment was this: "Sir, I must tell you I have worked telephones for the majority of my adult life and never have I heard phones answered in such an upbeat and pleasant manner. If the first voices you hear at a company are your first impressions of a company, you, sir, have a first-class company. You are to be congratulated on the quality and training of your personnel."

I mention this not to "toot our own horn," but simply to remind you that every time the phone rings at your company (or in your hand), it is an opportunity for someone to make either a good or a poor impression. Needless to say, you build business with good impressions. It's true that you have to follow through with the rest of it, but the start is important. In our computerized hurry-hurry world, I strongly urge you to train your people to assume that the next caller is the biggest account your company might ever land and they need to be pleasant, cheerful, courteous, and enthusiastic.

*Teacher to parent: "The good news is your child has a lot of creative ideas . . . The bad news is they are all in spelling."*

# I'M THE ONLY ONE WHO DOES ANYTHING AROUND HERE

*Deal as gently with the faults of others as you do with your own.*

CHINESE PROVERB

Several years ago I was to appear on a late-night television show in New York City. For some strange reason, they wanted me in the studio that afternoon at four thirty. I walked in and was stunned by the small size of the reception area. It contained a couch for three, a chair for one, a sink, a refrigerator, and a coffee maker.

As I sat down, a woman walked in, shook her head, and said, "Nobody makes any coffee except me!" She got busy and started a fresh pot of coffee. A few minutes later a guy walked in and, following the same procedure, said, "I can't believe it! This place would be a pigpen if it weren't for me! I'm the only person who ever does any cleanup." And he cleaned up the small area. Still later another woman walked in and complained, "Nobody ever puts anything up but me," and she proceeded to put things away.

All three of those people sincerely felt they were the only ones who ever did anything. Each one did a private halo adjustment in going through the process of making up, cleaning up, or putting up.

Question: Is that the way it is in your company, where "nobody does anything," but everyone thinks they are the only one who actually works? Thought: If that is true and you are the only one who does anything, think of the incredible advantage that gives you. Not only do you have job security, but you have unlimited opportunity to move up the ladder. However, if you have a chip on your shoulder, if you honestly feel that you do everything and you share that feeling with others, your bad attitude negates your good work. So stay busy, keep working, and smile about it. Your performance and good attitude about doing everything will catch up with you. You'll move up.

*It's hard to say when one generation ends and the next begins—but it's somewhere around 9 or 10 at night.*

EXECUTIVE SPEECHWRITER NEWSLETTER

# ONE BASKET AT A TIME

*Community should be spelled "come in unity."*

Many years ago when he was in East Asia, the late Bill Schiebler of Eden Prairie, Minnesota, had a unique experience. He was in farming country, where every inch of ground is important. A towering hill with a bamboo thicket on top was part of the terrain. The elders of the village decided that the hill needed to be removed for farming purposes. The American mind could not conceive of the hill being moved without the aid of giant earthmoving equipment, but the mindset and work ethic there were different.

Thousands of people who lived in the immediate area participated in the venture and even accepted it as a routine matter of their everyday life. Baskets of dirt were handed down from top to bottom, and in some cases, the lines were two miles long. It appeared as if nothing was happening; the hill did not seem to be going away. But over a period of time, because of incredible teamwork, the commitment of thousands of people, and a steady day-by-day involvement, the hill gradually diminished and the lower areas rose to a beautiful, flat farming area.

The Americans who witnessed the effort were astonished because the day came when no hill was left. They realized then that virtually any task can be accomplished when you get everyone on the same page, committed to a joint effort for the mutual benefit of all. Bill Schiebler wisely made the point that we should use this example for everyday living. When we are confronted with seemingly impossible tasks, if we break them down into small segments—or one basket at a time—we can literally accomplish the impossible and move those mountains. Note: the villagers took a liability (for farming purposes)—a mountain—and used that for dirt to create a valuable asset (rich farmland).

Think about it. Examine your liabilities—maybe you can convert them to assets, even if it's just a basket at a time.

*A prizefighter, floored in the second round by a powerful punch, tried to look up from the mat. "Let the referee count," yelled his trainer. "Don't get up until eight." The fighter nodded and replied weakly, "What time is it now?"*

*EXECUTIVE SPEECHWRITER NEWSLETTER*

# WHY YOU ARE WHERE YOU ARE

Choice—not chance—determines human destiny.

ROBERT W. ELLIS

Many years ago as a young, aspiring speaker, I heard an older speaker who was quite philosophical say that you are where you are because that's exactly where you want to be. I thought about his statement, decided it was the "wisdom of the ages," and verbalized it in my own presentations. Over a period of time, a series of events took place that convinced me his statement was not true in my case. I was broke, in debt, and down in the dumps. I wanted to be prosperous and excited about my future.

It came through loud and clear that I was where I was and what I was because of the decisions and choices I had made in my life. I made those choices based on the information I had, much of which was erroneous. The reality is if I'm given the wrong directions to go from point A to point

B, I'm not going to reach point B unless I change directions. It's equally true that if I'm given the wrong directions on how to move from being broke and in debt to being successful and prosperous, I'm not going to end up at the place I want to be.

One important decision you can make even as you read these words is to think about what Thomas Sikking said: "You're not the product of a broken home, a devastated economy, a world in the upheaval of war, a minority group, a family of drunkards, or a poverty-ridden neighborhood. You are the product of your own thinking processes and whatever you're thinking about today is the cornerstone of your tomorrow."

If someone else has abused you in the past, it's okay to give them credit for fouling up your past, but do not give them permission to ruin your present and your future. Take control of your thoughts and your future. Determine that you will have a better tomorrow.

*Being popular is important; otherwise*
*people might not like you.*

MIMI POND

# THE WINDOW OF OPPORTUNITY

There is an advantage in every disadvantage
and a gift in every problem.

JOHN JOHNSON

One Saturday I was in Tampa, Florida, for a seminar. At seven o'clock I stepped out of my hotel to do my walking but, unfortunately, it was raining. The good news is that there was a parking garage attached to the hotel, so I headed there to take my walk. Needless to say, I prefer to walk outdoors where I can see things as I go, but walking in a covered garage beats getting wet and certainly beats not walking at all. I had been enjoying my walk and planning my talk for about twenty-five minutes when I suddenly noticed that the rain had stopped. I hurried outside to take advantage of that window of opportunity and had made it about a block and a half when the rain returned. I headed back to the covered garage and continued my walk—and the planning of my talk.

As I reflect on my activity that morning, I had no idea how long it would continue to rain or how long the break in the rain would last. However, I do believe that too many people wait for everything to be "just right" before they do anything, and they often miss out on life's opportunities.

The second little lesson I learned on that walk is that in a parking garage you follow the incline to the top. It's more difficult to walk up, but to develop endurance you've got to go uphill. To go up in the business world or, for that matter, in the academic or political world, you frequently have to experience difficulty as you go. Without the difficulty you never develop the mental sharpness and physical strength necessary to succeed.

The only way to the mountaintop is through the valley. When you encounter those mountains, just remember that the climbing will enable you to climb the next one higher and faster.

*They say money doesn't go far these days, but it*
*sure manages to keep its distance from me!*

# THE HEART OF A CHAMPION

*It's not what the vision is, it's what the vision does.*

Some things cannot be measured, and the heart is one of them. I think of three former NFL stars. Mike Singletary, according to the experts, was too short and his forty-yard speed was not that great. However, they could not measure his heart and they did not measure his speed for the first five to fifteen yards, and at that distance he was exceptionally fast. As a result, when a running back would break through the line of scrimmage, instead of stopping him five to eight yards downfield as most linebackers do, Singletary was able to stop him in the first couple of yards. That made quite a difference.

Emmitt Smith's forty-yard speed was not earth-shattering either, and that caused him to be drafted later than he otherwise would have been. Again, the experts could not measure his heart or the burst of speed he was able to generate from the instant he touched the ball. As a result of both, he was able to break through the hole at the line and pick up those five to eight yards on a consistent basis and frequently break for much longer runs.

Jerry Rice is the other classic example. His forty-yard speed was also not record breaking, but his commitment to excellence and the fact that he was a game-player—meaning that once the chips were down he was at his best—were not measurable. Videotape of Jerry Rice shows him running stride for stride downfield with a defensive back until the pass is thrown to him. At that point, Jerry turns on the afterburners and frequently leaves the defensive back well behind.

There's something here for all of us to learn. Namely, we can measure IQ, speed, strength, and a host of other things, but the will to win and the commitment to excellence will enable a person of average ability to excel. So use what you've got—including your heart.

*You can't just go on being a good egg . . .*
*you must either hatch or go bad.*

C. S. LEWIS

# MOST OF US ARE PARROTS

*Without integrity no one listens. Without trust no one follows.*

In our society today we hear clichés and repeat them, whether they make sense or not. For example, Shakespeare said, "Nothing is either good or bad, but thinking makes it so." A moment's reflection will convince you that thinking has nothing to do with whether rape or murder is good or bad. Those acts are bad. Many people today say, "Well, everything is relative," which is also absurd. We must have some absolutes in life; otherwise, obeying the law is relative. There are several thousand laws on the books, so let's go down the list and choose the ones that are relative to us and, consequently, obey only them. Chaos would be the obvious result.

For the eighty-five-year-old, driving forty miles per hour might seem far too fast, while ninety miles per hour for the seventeen-year-old might not seem fast at all. A "bump" by a 300-pound NFL offensive lineman on a 290-pound defensive end would be relatively insignificant. The same force applied against a frail senior citizen could result in serious consequences.

As you ponder things of this nature, I believe you will come to the conclusion that the more things we make relative, the more chaos we're going to have in our society. It's safe to say that virtually every husband and wife in America does not want their mate to be "relatively" faithful. Most of us have even taken vows that being relative has nothing to do with. We're going to love, cherish, honor, and be faithful to our spouse. Add relativity and referencing good or bad to that vow, and very few marriages would survive.

The list is endless, but I encourage you to eliminate much of this relativity stuff and this idea that "nothing is either good or bad but thinking makes it so" approach to life. Follow the moral absolutes that have stood civilization in good stead for several thousand years.

*Why is it that what you hear is never quite as interesting as what you overhear?*

# INTELLIGENT SELFISHNESS

*A person is no greater than their dreams, ideals, hopes, and plans. A person dreams the dream and dreams of fulfilling it. It's the dream that makes the person.*

*Fortune* magazine published an intriguing article on a multibillionaire from Hong Kong named Li Ka-shing. His two sons, Victor and Richard, were raised in their father's business, attending board meetings and conferences where they were instructed, informed, and indoctrinated in their father's philosophy.

Obviously, if you're worth a few billion dollars, you have a different approach to your children from the one most of us would take. For example, how do you explain to a nine-year-old that he can't have a bicycle that costs $250 because it's too expensive when that nine-year-old has already observed that money is not a concern within the household? But Li Ka-shing recognized that affording it was not the issue; teaching sound principles was the idea involved. For that reason, he kept a reasonably close rein on indulgences for his sons. Traditionally, youngsters growing up in extraordinarily wealthy families, not newly rich athletes or movie stars but those whose fortunes have been in the family for several generations, are familiar with financial restraint.

Perhaps the most intriguing thing Richard observed as he watched his father, who was truly an entrepreneurial genius, was that his dad engaged in many joint ventures with people who had products and ideas but were short on capital. Richard learned that if 10 percent is a fair percentage of the business you receive as a result of your investment, but you know you can get 11 percent, it is wise to take only 9 percent. Li Ka-shing taught his boys that if he took less than he could get, countless other people with good ideas and good products but no money would flock to his doorstep. The net result is that instead of making one profitable—albeit greedy—deal, he could make numerous good, solid deals at the lower percentage, and the total amount of profits would be dramatically higher. That's being intelligently selfish, which is really unselfish and wise.

*A hypocrite has been accurately described*
*as one who is not himself on Sunday.*

# THE POWER OF THE WORD

A committee is a group of people who individually
can do nothing but collectively meet and
decide that nothing can be done.

FRED ALLEN

Frequently, we become so pragmatic that we fail to be effective. Years ago the editor of the *Dallas Morning News* pointed out to the sportswriters that "Bill" was not a suitable substitute for "William," and "Charlie" was not a suitable substitute for "Charles." Taking him literally, one of the sportswriters in the heyday of Doak Walker of Southern Methodist University wrote about an important game. In his story he pointed out that in the third quarter Doak Walker had left the game with a "Charles horse." I think you'll agree that the story lost some meaning with the use of "Charles."

Perhaps the ultimate absurdity occurred in an article in a national publication when the writer set up the computer to analyze Lincoln's Gettysburg Address. Incidentally, that address contains 362 words and 302 of them are one syllable. It's simple and direct but powerful and effective.

The computer, however, made some recommendations about how the speech really should have been given. For example, instead of saying, "Four score and seven years," the computer suggested, "Eighty-seven years." The efficiency in the reduction is obvious, but the loss of effectiveness, power, drama, and passion is even more obvious. When Lincoln said, "We are engaged in a great civil war," the computer questioned whether the word *great* was justified. This despite the fact that our nation suffered more than 640,000 casualties, including more than 364,000 deaths. The computer stated that the sentences were too long, and it criticized the statement that we could never forget what happened at Gettysburg as being negative. I think you'll agree that eloquence and drama, combined with passion, logic, and common sense, are far more effective at inspiring people to do great things than technical correctness could be.

Think about it. Knowing their power, use your words carefully. You'll be a greater contributor to humankind.

*Midwinter note received by the weather bureau: "Have just shoveled two feet of partly cloudy off my driveway."*

# A BEAR IN A TREE

Concern should drive us into action and not into a depression.

PYTHAGORUS

Several years ago at dusk, just outside Keithville, Louisiana, someone spotted a black bear in a tree. Word quickly spread around the little town, and many of the citizens gathered to see him. The local veterinarian provided a dart gun loaded with drugs to sedate the bear. Concern was raised that he might fall out of the tree and injure himself, so the fire department was called and their net was put in place to catch him.

A bonfire was built and all night long they tried to get that bear out of the tree. It seemed he was oblivious to the crowd, and apparently the drugs were having no effect on him because no bear came tumbling down.

Then came the dawn and they could more clearly see that "bear" in the tree. The bear turned out to be a black plastic bag filled with garbage. No one ever figured out how that garbage bag got to the top of the tree.

Unfortunately, many people live with a "bear up their tree" and allow it to affect their lives in a harmful way. When they learn the truth, they discover the "bear" is negative garbage that has been dumped in their minds over a period of time by music, television, and "friends," as well as the general public. The good news is that, regardless of their age, a person can get that "bear" out of their tree by bringing it to the light of day—as they did in Keithville, Louisiana. Simply by reversing the process and putting good, clean, pure, powerful, and positive information into their mind, a person can bury that "old garbage." I've seen numerous people who follow that procedure dramatically improve their lives. You can do the same thing.

*A big-game hunter today is a fellow who switches channels all Sunday afternoon during football season.*

# WHAT DO YOU EXPECT?

You get better results if you have high expectations. This is true in science, math, reading, football, or band.

CHARLES ADAIR

Speaker and author Mamie McCullough tells this story. Several years ago as she started the school year, second-grade teacher Frances Hurst of Rayville Parish, Rayville, Louisiana, was told that she had the "middle" class of students. At that time, all the students were grouped as either "low," "middle," or "high." This grouping or grading bothered Ms. Hurst quite a bit because she had never taught ability grouping before. On her first day of class, the students told her they were the middle group, and at that point Ms. Hurst went into action. She closed the door, placed paper over the glass in the windows, and told the students there had been a mistake and that they were actually the high group.

From that point on, she treated them as though they were the high group. Her expectations for them were high; their own expectations and confidence grew, and at the end of the school year, the SRA test (which is given to measure the achievement for each group) revealed that her group had tested one year ahead of the high group. Since this test was a class average, that meant that some of the students were testing much higher than the high group.

Someone once said that if you treat a person as he is, you make him worse than he was, but if you treat that person as the individual he's capable of becoming, you make him the best person possible. That's a marvelous philosophy because it's true. This was aptly proved by Ms. Frances Hurst. Wouldn't it be wonderful if every parent, teacher, and employer in America would treat everybody as if they were in the high group? Odds are dramatic that everything would be better. You can't influence everybody, but you can influence those you work and live with. Put them all in the high group—they'll climb higher and so will you.

*You can't go against the grain of the universe*
*and not expect to get splinters.*

C. S. LEWIS

# THE EDSEL WAS AN OUTSTANDING SUCCESS

God looks for growth, not perfection, so our
objective is excellence, not perfection.

You may recall that the Edsel automobile produced by the Ford Motor Company was, in the view of the buying public, a dismal failure. Tens of millions of dollars were lost; it was the butt of numerous jokes and was soon in the graveyard of cars that did not make it.

The rest of the story, however, is quite different. You fail not when you're beaten but when you quit. The Ford Motor Company—as you know—did not quit. As a matter of fact, out of the Edsel came incredible success. Some of the technology subsequently developed and the research that followed enabled the company to produce the Mustang, which was Ford's all-time bestseller and most profitable motorcar. From what the engineers learned on the Mustang, they were able to produce the Taurus, and for several years the Taurus was the number-one-selling car in America.

The key to all of this is that when we make a mistake—and all of us periodically do—we should make it a point to ask, What can I learn to change this temporary failure into a resounding success? That's the beginning point of doing great things. We never really reach our full potential until we've been tested and tried. Traditionally, the team that takes the toughest route to the Super Bowl, challenging and beating the toughest teams, is the one that wins the Super Bowl.

Message: when adversity is staring you in the face and you fail in an endeavor, look at it as a learning experience. That's what Ford did. That's why the Edsel was ultimately such a success in the overall scope of things. Adjust your thinking to that approach, and you will convert your "Edsels" to successes.

*This country is so urbanized we think low-fat milk comes from cows on aerobic exercise programs.*

P. J. O'ROURKE

# EDUCATION IS IMPORTANT

It's in the struggle itself that you define yourself.

PAT BUCHANAN

Albert Einstein said, "It is essential that the student acquire an understanding of and a lively feeling for values. He must acquire a vivid sense of the beautiful and of the morally good, otherwise he—with a specialized knowledge—more closely resembles a well-trained dog than a harmoniously developed person." Daniel Webster said, "Knowledge does not comprise all which is contained in the large term of education. The feelings are to be disciplined, the passions are to be restrained, true and worthy motives are to be inspired, a profound religious feeling is to be instilled, and pure morality inculcated under all circumstances. All this is comprised in education."

James Truslow Adams said there are obviously two educations: one should teach us how to make a living and the other how to live. In order to acquire both educations, three things are necessary: we need information, knowledge, and wisdom. We get information out of newspapers, magazines, and the internet. We acquire knowledge through good books, lectures and seminars, and also from online. But these first two will not give us both types of education. If information and knowledge were the complete answer, every PhD in America would be rich and happy, and every high school dropout would be broke and miserable. Obviously, this is not true.

The third dimension of education is wisdom. Wisdom is the correct use of the truth in the knowledge we have. Wisdom enables us to take information and knowledge and use it to make good decisions. On a personal level, my mother finished only the fifth grade, was widowed in the heart of the Great Depression, and had six children too young to work. Obviously, she needed wisdom to use the knowledge she had to make right decisions to successfully raise her family. Fortunately, she had the wisdom that comes from God, which James spoke of in his epistle: "If any of you lacks wisdom, let him ask of God, who gives to all liberally and without reproach, and it will be given to him" (1:5 NKJV).

*There aren't nearly enough crutches in*
*the world for all the lame excuses.*

MARCUS STROUP

# IS GUILT GOOD OR BAD?

*To forgive is to overlook an offense and treat the offender as not guilty.*

WEBSTER'S DICTIONARY (1828)

If you follow trials in our courtrooms on a regular basis, you know that after the judge has passed sentence, he will read one of two statements. If the criminal is given a sentence lighter than the crime seemed to warrant, the statement will frequently include the fact that the perpetrator of the crime was genuinely remorseful and had a deep sense of guilt for the wrong done, so the judge believes the criminal will not be a threat to society.

On the other hand, if the sentence is the maximum for the crime, the judge, the arresting officers, and others will say the accused had absolutely no remorse, felt no guilt, and "we believe they will repeat this crime."

The dictionary says that *guilt* is the "fact of being

responsible for an offense or wrongdoing; the disposition to break the law." It is "guilty behavior and remorseful awareness of having done something wrong."

Were it not for the feeling of guilt, anarchy would exist. Merited guilt serves some useful functions in our society. Unmerited guilt, which is imposed upon us by someone else for an imagined wrong, can be destructive and debilitating. Merited guilt is closely akin to empathy, which enables us to, in a real sense, feel the way the victim feels. As a result, we are more likely to deal more sensitively with that person in the future. If we, as wrongdoers, have no sense of remorse, chances are excellent that we will repeat the action and further damage the individual and destroy any possibility of a reconciliation or a permanent relationship.

Message: The next time you feel guilty about something, analyze it and if it is merited guilt, get excited—because that means you're on the way to being a better person. If it's unmerited guilt, simply reject it and go on with your life.

*Overheard in a courtroom: Said the judge to the accused, "My inclination is to find you guilty, but hey, who am I to judge?"*

# GROW/SWELL

Our ego is our silent partner—too often
with a controlling interest.

CULLEN HIGHTOWER

As a rookie salesman I had a very difficult time getting started. However, once the ball started rolling, I enjoyed a spectacular four-year run of success. This led to a career change and new job in New York City. It was exciting and rewarding but required that I leave home each morning before my two little girls were awake, and most of the time when I returned at night, they were already asleep. I could not handle that style of parenting, so in just three months' time we moved back to Columbia, South Carolina.

I got into a promotional-type business and temporarily enjoyed some success that quickly evaporated. At that point I stopped growing and started swelling, which led to sixteen additional job and career changes within the following five years. I became a super-critic, a know-it-all, and a very difficult person to work with. One of the companies I briefly worked for was an insurance company that had been in business for many years. This astonished me because they were obviously way behind the times and I had some absolutely brilliant ideas that would revolutionize their business and expand their market share. They rejected these very significant ideas. I left in a huff, wondering how they would ever survive—which, incidentally, they did.

After five frustrating years I finally had a reality check and realized that the success I enjoyed earlier had come because I had completely committed myself to improving what I did instead of assuming I knew it all. I made a strong commitment to the new company I represented and worked hard and enthusiastically, while continually acquiring new information from those who had beaten many a path before I came along. Interestingly enough, results were excellent and progress was steady so that just two years later I was back on a career path that has been most rewarding and satisfying.

I hope the message is clear. Keep growing. Don't start swelling.

*EGO stands for "Edging God Out."*

**WAYNE DYER**

# TRY IT—MAYBE YOU CAN

*Everyone hears only what he understands.*

JOHANN WOLFGANG VON GOETHE

I love the story of the ninety-year-old lady who, when asked if she could play the piano, responded that she didn't know. "What do you mean, you don't know?" she was asked. The lady smilingly replied, "I've never tried." That's a good answer that I hope will open some eyes, ears, and thinking. Many of us have talents we've never benefited from because we have never tried to do a specific thing.

Music lovers still recognize the name of Nat King Cole. He was universally admired for his beautiful, silky-smooth voice. He could sing ballads as few have ever done. What many people do not realize is that he started his career as a piano player. One night in a West Coast club, the featured singer was ill and the owner demanded to know where he was. When Cole responded that he was sick, the club owner said, "If we don't have a singer there'll be no check." That night Nat King Cole became a singer. The rest is history.

For the first seven years of his career, Will Rogers performed rope tricks. He was a genuine cowboy and very much a "man's man." He held the attention of the audience with the rope tricks he performed. One night someone in the audience asked him a question. His candid response brought a considerable amount of laughter. Then someone else asked a question and Rogers's response again was humorous. That night his career as a full-scale humorist was launched. But he was far more than a humorist. He had the homespun wisdom that not only encouraged and entertained but also gave people information and inspiration they could use in their everyday lives.

Message: you might not be able to carry a tune, do rope tricks, or give humorous, homespun advice, but you do have a song to sing and ability that needs to be developed and used.

Suggestion: The next time someone asks if you can do something you've never done before, don't automatically respond "no." Think about it. Maybe you should give it a try. Who knows? Maybe you have talents you've never recognized.

*In the town I was raised in, things moved so*
*slowly it took two hours to watch 60 Minutes.*

KEN DAVIS

# MY MOST UNFORGETTABLE CHARACTER

Love your enemies. Without them you'd probably
have nobody to blame but yourself.

The Eartha White story appeared in *Reader's Digest* many years ago. She was the four-and-a-half-foot-tall daughter of a former slave. She believed that "service is the price we pay for the space we occupy on this planet." She lived by the principle that each of us should do all the good we can in all the ways we can in all the places we can for all the people we can while we can.

Miss Eartha gave up a promising opera career to join her mother in trying to make things easier for the people who came to her mother's free soup kitchen. She taught school for sixteen years, then used her small savings to open a department store that catered primarily to African Americans. She eventually started a team laundry, an employment agency, a real estate company, and an insurance business. She amassed an estate worth more than $1 million, only to commit most of it to projects that made her a one-woman welfare department.

Her life was about helping people. She reached down and lifted those who needed a hand up instead of a handout. She maintained a boarding home for indigents and a mercy hospital for those who had become completely helpless. At another house she took in unwed mothers, and in another she nursed alcoholics back to sobriety. She also donated buildings for two childcare centers and turned a vacant movie house into a recreation center for children who lived in slums. Her deep faith led her to quote John 15:7, which says, "If ye abide in me, and my words abide in you, ye shall ask what ye will, and it shall be done unto you" (KJV).

She worked hard, lived expectantly, and died fulfilled. If each of us did a fraction of what she did, the contribution to society would be significant. The sheer joy of giving and doing for others is hard to top. Take action. Follow Eartha White's example, and the road to the top will be smoother.

*A sign at the beginning of the serving line in front of the apples at a church picnic: "God is watching, take only one." At the end of the line next to the cookies, a little sign said, "Take as many as you want. God is busy watchin' the apples."*

# PERSONALITY OR CHARACTER?

Reputation is what folks think you are. Personality is what you seem to be. Character is what you really are.

John Maxwell, one of the top leadership authorities in America, says that most people would rather work on their personality than on their character, and how right he is. Perhaps that is because personality development brings more immediate rewards, is less demanding, and, in most cases, involves little sacrifice on our part. Personality development involves learning new conversational skills, style, or developing a speaking ability.

The development of character is more profound, is considerably more difficult, and often involves making changes that are at least temporarily uncomfortable and often very demanding. Changing habits is always a difficult procedure. The development of virtues also requires time because it means we must discipline some of our appetites and passions. Keeping promises and being sensitive to the feelings and convictions of others are not things that most of us do naturally. We have to work at them. Character development is the best indication of maturity.

Yes, it is more difficult to develop character than personality and yes, it's true that the rewards are not as immediate. However, the long-term rewards are infinitely greater. To value oneself is important, but to be able at the same time to subordinate yourself to higher purposes and principles is the paradoxical essence of highest humanity, and it is the foundation for effective leadership. I believe I'm safe in saying that in today's world, the need for character and leadership outweighs the need for more people with more personality. Fortunately, when you develop the character, the personality develops far more easily and more naturally.

*Good times reveal part of your character;*
*tough times reveal all of it.*

# HANDLING CRITICISM

No one so thoroughly appreciates the value of
constructive criticism as the one who's giving it.

HAL CHADWICK

The late comedian Groucho Marx said, "Whatever it is, I'm against it." My dictionary says that *criticism* is "the art of judging with propriety of the beauties and faults of a performance; remark on beauties and faults; critical observation, verbal or written."

Colonel George Washington Goethals, the man who completed the Panama Canal, handled criticism effectively. During the construction he had numerous problems with the geography, climate, and mosquitoes. As with all mammoth projects, he had his critics back home who constantly harped on what he was doing and predicted that he would never complete the project. However, he stuck to the task and said nothing. One day an associate asked him, "Aren't you going to answer the critics?" "Yes," Goethals responded. "How?" he was asked. "With the canal," Goethals replied. Though that approach didn't bring instant satisfaction, the canal itself brought long-term vindication.

Aristotle said criticism was meant as a standard of judging will. Addison said it was ridiculous for any man to criticize the works of another if he has not distinguished himself by his own performance.

The world is hard on critics, but on occasion they have real value. Ask yourself this question: What interest does this person (critic) have in me? A parent, teacher, employer, or coach has a vested interest in your performance. Unfortunately, many of them do not know how to effectively build up a person while giving suggestions that can make a difference. The key is to criticize the performance and not the performer. My mother once criticized my performance by saying, "For most boys this would be all right. But you're not most boys—you're my son and my son can do better than that." She had "criticized the performance" because it needed improvement, but she had praised the performer because he needed the praise.

*Honest criticism is hard to take, particularly*
*when it comes from a relative, a friend,*
*an acquaintance, or a stranger.*

FRANKLIN P. JONES

# ANYTHING CAN HAPPEN—
# AND IT USUALLY DOES

The critic sees a problem to point it out and
establish his authority or expertise. The coach sees
a problem in order to work on it and improve it.

FRED SMITH

One of the clichés in professional athletics is that on any
given day in any given city, one professional athletic team
can beat another team. Their standings in the win-loss
record at that moment don't really matter. That's equally
true in individual competition with players who are skilled
and determined to do their best.

Tennis player Kathy Horvath had every reason to believe
that she would lose when she faced Martina Navratilova
on May 28, 1983. Kathy was rated forty-fifth in the world;
Martina was ranked number one, had won thirty-six
straight matches, and had not lost a match all year. Her

record in 1982 was ninety victories with only three defeats. Her defeats were to highly ranked players such as Chris Evert Lloyd and Pam Shriver. Furthermore, Kathy Horvath was only seventeen years old, and they were playing in front of sixteen thousand people.

As it often happens in such matches, Kathy got off to a fast start and won the first set 6–4. Martina came storming back in the second set and blew her off the court, winning that set 6–0. They started the last set, and it was truly nip and tuck. They were tied at 3–3, and Martina was serving. To everyone's surprise, Kathy, the overwhelming underdog, won the set and the match. Someone asked Kathy about her strategy, and she replied, "I was playing to win."

That's significant. Too many people play not to lose; Kathy Horvath was playing to win. I urge you to play to win.

*Baseball manager Casey Stengel to catcher Joe Garagiola: "Joe, when they list all the great catchers, you'll be there listening."*

# MEMORY IS IMPORTANT

*Be like an eraser—recognize your mistakes, learn from your mistakes, and then erase them from your memory.*

When someone wonders if I remember such and such an event or so-and-so, if the answer is no, one of my favorite responses is to smile and acknowledge that no, I don't. Then I explain that I have a brilliant memory—it's just awfully short.

The truth is, memory is the key to many things. If we don't remember things, we are hopelessly lost and are placed in a confinement of sorts. However, there are some things you can do effective immediately that will improve your memory substantially. Douglas Herrmann, PhD, in his book *Super Memory*, points out that practice alone can improve "global" memory and substantially boost retrieval ability in certain areas of life. He says when you practice specific memory tasks, you can produce spectacular results.

According to Dr. Herrmann, most people who attempt

to learn a long string of numbers read to them normally will remember about seven of the numbers correctly. However, after practicing for several months, many people can remember forty, fifty, sixty, or even as many as eighty numbers in a string. The only problem is that it does require some work and a commitment to the objective.

Dr. Herrmann points out that most people can recall about a third of what they know. However, after a month of daily practicing to recall specific bits of information, they can dramatically improve, whether it's remembering a geographical location, a historical fact, or a personal event that took place many years earlier. This proves that if we do have a "poor memory," it's probably caused by an untrained or lazy memory. Work on that memory. You'll have more fun and be more effective, more productive, and happier in the process.

*If you want to test your memory, try to recall what you were worrying about one year ago today.*

E. JOSEPH COSSMAN

# THE FULLY EQUIPPED COW

Great things are accomplished with slow movement.
Nothing is accomplished by standing still.

The story is told about a farmer who went into an automobile dealership to buy a stripped-down model and ended up with all the bells and whistles. The $14,000 standard car turned into a $22,000 luxury vehicle. He loved all the extras, but frankly, he had exceeded his budget. A few months later he had a chance to at least partially balance the scale. The salesman who sold him the car showed up at his farm to buy a cow. After carefully looking the herd over, he made his choice and asked, "How much?"

The farmer pleasantly replied that the price was $395. The salesman was pleased and said he would take the cow. The farmer went into his shed, figured the details, came back out, and presented the salesman with the bill totaling $920.20. Needless to say, the salesman responded with some feeling, "But I thought you told me the price was $395!"

The farmer assured him that was the price of the standard cow, but this one came equipped with a two-tone genuine leather cowhide cover for an additional $95. There was an extra stomach built in to increase capacity and performance, which was $110. The attached flyswatter was $35, and at $15 each the four milk dispensers came to an extra $60. The colorful dual horns at $20 each came to $40, and the automatic fertilizer plant, guaranteed for life, was another $125, for a total of $465. The tax was $60.20, so the total bill was $920.20.

I'm certain many of you, as you read this, feel a degree of empathy with the farmer. Maybe the smile you get from the story and the fact that you can share it with others will reduce some of the pain that goes, on occasion, with over-spending your budget. Go ahead. Have a good laugh. Share it with others.

*The last thing my kids ever did to earn*
*money was lose their baby teeth.*

PHYLLIS DILLER, "ROD'S PONDERS," MAY 16, 1994

# BUSY BUT POLITE

The first responsibility of a leader is to define reality.
The last is to say thank you. In between the two
the leader must become a servant and a debtor.
That sums up the progress of an artful leader.

MAX DE PREE

Theodore Roosevelt, former president of the United States, has been described as founder of the Bull Moose Party, the man who led his troops up San Juan Hill in the Spanish-American War, a big-game hunter, a family man, a civil servant, and a host of other things.

His life story would indicate that he was not only an extraordinarily successful man but surely one of the busiest and best-organized ever. However, with all of his busyness, even during his campaign trips when the demands on his time were the greatest, he still retained some of those human qualities that made him so successful. Simple example: he never forgot to thank others who did things for him. On his whistle-stop tours during his campaign trips, he always left his private car to stop and thank the engineer and fireman for a safe and comfortable trip. True, it took only a few minutes of his time, but when your minutes are so few, they are quite important. However, Roosevelt felt that those minutes were well-invested, and he enjoyed meeting the people who had served him so well. In the process he made friends for life. Doing simple little things, thinking of the other person, endeared him to people all across America, which certainly was a significant reward for the few minutes it took him to say thank-you.

Someone once said that you could always tell a "big" man by the way he treated a "little" man. By that yardstick alone you would have to agree that Theodore Roosevelt was a "big" man. Message: Take time to be kind and to say thank-you. The returns can be great.

*Two ways to make every day a better day: think and thank.*

# A TIMELESS TRUTH

It's one of the most beautiful compensations of this life that no man can sincerely try to help another without helping himself.

RALPH WALDO EMERSON

While going through my files, I came across a blurb from *Catholic Digest* written by Mary Kinsolving, which is as relevant today as it was many years ago when it was written. Ms. Kinsolving tells a story of living in Manhattan where, as a child, her mother walked her to school four blocks away every morning and then walked home with her again in the afternoon. One hard winter her mother came down with pneumonia and Mary had to go to school and return home by herself. She states that on the way home the second day she fell on some ice while crossing the street, and at that moment a car skidded toward her and came within inches of her before it stopped. "The driver helped me up," she said, "and I managed to get home but didn't tell my mother because I didn't want her to worry."

The next morning the streets were even icier, and when she came to her first cross street, Mary was terrified and stood at the intersection for a long time. Finally, an elderly woman came over to her and said, "I don't see very well. May I hold your hand when I cross the street?" She replied, "Oh, yes," and the elderly lady took her hand and "before long we were on the other side." Then Mary Kinsolving walked a short distance and looked back to see how the woman was doing. To her surprise, "She was crossing the street we had just crossed together and was walking by herself much faster than we had before." Ms. Kinsolving then realized that the lady had pretended poor eyesight only to help her cross the street. Much later in life she understood that she could overcome her own fears by helping someone else.

What marvelous advice from years gone past!

*It is pretty hard to tell what does brings happiness;*
*poverty and wealth have both failed.*

KIN HUBBARD

# WHY WORRY?

*Life is much like Christmas. You're more apt to*
*get what you expect than what you want.*

Worry has been described as "interest paid on trouble before it comes due." One of America's worst enemies is worry. Worry is like a rocking chair; it requires a lot of energy, and it gets you nowhere. Leo Buscaglia said, "Worry never robs tomorrow of its sorrow. It only saps today of its joy."

Question: Are you a worrier? Americans take more pills to forget more worries about more things than ever before and more than people in any other nation in history. That's bad. According to Dr. Charles Mayo, "Worry affects the circulation and the whole nervous system. I've never known a man who died from overwork, but I've known many who have died from doubt." Doubt always creates worry, and in most cases, lack of information raises the doubt.

Mathematically speaking, it really doesn't make sense to worry. Psychologists and other researchers tell us that roughly 40 percent of what we worry about will never happen and 30 percent has already happened. Additionally, 12 percent of our worries are over unfounded health concerns. Another 10 percent of our worries involve the daily miscellaneous fretting that accomplishes nothing. That leaves only 8 percent. Plainly speaking, Americans are worrying 92 percent of the time for no good reason, and if Dr. Mayo is right, it's killing us.

One solution that will reduce your worry is this: don't worry about what you can't change. Example: For a number of years I've flown in excess of two hundred thousand miles a year. On occasion, flights are canceled or delayed. I wrote this while sitting on a runway waiting for the gate to clear. If I worried or became angry, nothing would have changed. If I took constructive action and finished this chapter instead, I would be ahead of the game. That's a positive way to use the energy that I would have wasted on anger, frustration, or worrying.

The message is clear: if you don't like your situation in life, don't fret or worry—do something about it. Worry less, and act more.

*To people who want to be rich and famous, I'd say,*
*"Get rich first and see if that doesn't cover it."*

**BILL MURRAY**

# YOU'VE FAILED—NOW SIT DOWN

One of the ironies of life is that at the very moment
we're teaching our children to walk we must also be
teaching them to walk away; that while we nourish the
roots we must also help them spread their wings.

*EXECUTIVE SPEECHWRITER NEWSLETTER*

Most parents experience the joy of watching their children turn over, then crawl, then stand up, and then take those first steps. With outstretched arms they stand two or three steps away and encourage the little one to come to them. Chances are about three trillion to one that when the baby falls down the parent is not going to say, "Okay, you had your chance—you blew it! So don't you ever try to walk again!" That's absurd, but isn't it equally absurd to think we can accomplish major things in our lives without experiencing reversals of some kind? We all need to remember that failure is an event, not a person, that success is a process and not just an instant happening. Few succeed overnight. Instead, they succeed over time.

Troy Aikman, Steve Young, Brett Favre, and Dan Marino were all extremely effective NFL quarterbacks and yet each of the four threw more incomplete passes than 99 percent of all the quarterbacks who ever threw a football. Obviously, along the way they also threw an awful lot of completions.

The top salesperson in the organization probably missed more sales than 90 percent of the salespeople on the team, but they also made more calls than the others made. There's never been a doctor who served many patients who, despite their best efforts, did not lose some of them to death. But they understood that was part of life itself.

All of us need to remember there is a vast difference between failing in an event and failing in life. Once we understand that, our chances for success substantially increase. We need to remember that winners are people who got up one more time than they were knocked down.

*Failure is the path of least persistence.*

# ECONOMIC NEED AND CRIME

Character is not made by crisis, it is only exhibited.

ROBERT FREEMAN

For years I have heard on television and read in newspapers that a poor person who could not find a job was, if not expected to turn to crime, at least excused for doing so. Unfortunately, the more this idea is promoted, the more likely it is to occur, especially among those who do not have a strong character base. The facts concerning this issue are interesting, and as a friend of mine was inclined to say, "Everyone is entitled to his own opinion, but no one is entitled to the wrong facts."

I was raised during the Great Depression, so I was familiar with an occasional knock at the back door by someone asking for something to eat in exchange for some work they could do around the house or garden. Interestingly enough, virtually no one asked for free food—they wanted to work for it instead. Statistics clearly validate that the crime rate coming out of the Depression was actually lower than it was when we entered the Depression.

An article in the *Financial Post* by David Frum points out that an identical situation occurred in Canada in the early 1990s. He stated that statistics confirmed that there was "an overall five percent drop" in criminality between 1992 and 1993. This, despite the fact that 1993 should have seen an increase in crime. Instead, faced with plant closures, job losses, and shrinking social services, Canadians became less inclined to break into houses and steal from the owners. The reality is that people do what they're taught and expected to do. If we will eliminate the concept that poverty breeds crime and more carefully teach that the right way is the best way, we will see further reductions in crime. In many cases an economic belt-tightening is a character-building experience that helps us learn to get along without many of the so-called necessities of life, so we emerge from the economic challenges stronger and better prepared to build a more successful future.

*About the only thing that can lie down on
the job and produce results is a hen.*

# GIVE WHAT YOU'VE GOT

There's only one way to succeed in anything
and that is to give it everything.

VINCE LOMBARDI

Agnes W. Thomas told the story of what happened when her
next-door neighbor died and left a fourteen-year-old daughter named Amy, who was often alone when her father was
at work. "Amy spent much of her after-school time in my
apartment, so I decided to teach her how to crochet.

"Over the years we spent many happy hours together as
we worked. One Christmas we called a local nursing home
and asked if they had any residents who would not be receiving gifts at Christmas. Amy and I took our crocheted lap
robes to these people on Christmas Eve.

"The following year Amy married and moved away, and
later when she came back to our area with her beautiful,
red-haired baby girl, she called and asked if I planned to

visit the nursing home on Christmas Eve. 'I want to be with you,' she said, 'but I haven't had any time to crochet since Jennifer was born, so I don't have any gifts to take them.' 'That's all right,' I said, 'you can help me take mine.' 'No, I have a better idea,' she said, 'I'll take my greatest treasure—my baby.'

"Great merriment appeared on the faces of the elderly people when we walked into the room with that beautiful baby. 'Oh, she looks just like my daughter did when she was a baby,' exclaimed one of the residents. 'May I hold her?' asked another. Jennifer was passed around like a doll. That baby brought more joy and laughter than all of my crocheted lap robes. Amy was happy too. 'They really liked my baby, didn't they?' she asked as we left the building. 'To make people happy, I guess you just give what you have.'"

How true. The human spirit is encouraged by the love and concern of another person, and what could be more encouraging and delightful to the elderly than holding an innocent baby? That's a real gift any time of the year.

*I may give out, but I'll never give up.*

RICHARD OVERTON

# THE HAWK AND THE SPARROW

The instant you set a goal a light goes on in your future.

JIM PALUCH

This morning I spotted a large hawk in the willow tree behind my home. There were two or three small birds, which I believe were sparrows, driving that hawk nuts! He would get comfortably situated and one of them would dive at him, quickly followed by another. The hawk moved three or four times, but those little birds continued to harass him until he took off for parts unknown. As I watched this little drama, I was reminded of the difference between the hawk and the eagle. When the eagle is chased by his enemies, instead of ignoring them or trying to avoid them, he flies straight toward the sun. He has special coverings on his eyes that enable him to look directly at the sun one moment and in the next instant drop his eyes and spot a field mouse far below. He is safe when he heads for the light.

We can relate this example to men and women. "Little" people—and I do not refer to size—are easily harassed by small incidents in life, bugged by every criticism, and angered at barbs from others. They squirm and become defensive, but this only encourages the barb-throwers to keep after them. Men and women of integrity, however, who are confident within themselves, are not affected by what the "little" people say about them. Like the eagle, they hide from their enemies in the light because they know who they are and what they stand for. They understand that with integrity they have nothing to fear because they have nothing to hide. Hopefully, the parallel is clear and there's a lesson there we can learn. Live with integrity; hide in the light.

*If you're in debt, cheer up and sing. Remember that the birds have bills and that's what they do.*

# SCHOOL VERSUS FINISHING EDUCATION

Those who have not distinguished themselves at school
need not on that account be discouraged. The greatest
minds do not necessarily ripen the quickest.

JOHN LUBBOCK

There's an old saying that you can finish school and even make it easy. That simply is not true of education. You never finish, and it is seldom easy, but it's always important.

Myrtle Estella Shannon did both—acquired an education and finished school. It's true that she was ninety-one before she finished college, and seven decades had passed since she was a teenager, but Ms. Shannon received her Bachelor of Arts on Sunday, January 21, 1996. She was still spry with a great sense of humor and a large amount of enthusiasm.

Hers is an inspiring story of an African American woman, raised in Vicksburg, Mississippi, at a time when members of her race were denied educational, social, and business opportunities. Her family eventually moved to Gary, Indiana, and still later to Chicago. She finished high school at sixteen, went on to business trade school when she was twenty, and earned a certificate in liberal arts from an adult education program at the University of Chicago when she was forty-seven. She started part-time at Roosevelt University in 1984 but had to stop in 1992 for cataract surgery. She returned to Roosevelt in 1995 to complete her final class for a degree.

Ms. Shannon always sat up front so she could be in the midst of intellectual discussions and because she could see and hear better. She was an above-average student, took some difficult courses, and did well in them. During the years when she was not in school, she traveled abroad and collected mementos to remind her of a fulfilled life.

It's hard to understand how Ms. Shannon was able to persist for so many years when she had many opportunities to decide that it really wasn't worth the effort. But aren't we glad she finished, and isn't she a marvelous example for all of us to follow?

*Every time you graduate from the school of experience, somebody thinks up a new course.*

# THE RESPONSIBILITY IS YOURS

You are the only person who can use your ability. That is an awesome responsibility because as a steward of your talent and ability, you have no options. You have been entrusted with something that you alone can develop and use.

Abraham Lincoln said, "You cannot escape the responsibility of tomorrow by evading it today." The blame game goes back to the beginning. God told Adam and Eve when He placed them in the garden that they could have it all, except they were not to eat the fruit of the tree in the middle of the garden.

However, they ate the fruit of that tree, and in the evening, as God walked in the garden, He called for Adam and Adam responded, "Over here, Lord." Then God asked the question, "Adam, did you eat the fruit of the tree in the middle of the garden?" God already knew the answer but He wanted Adam to respond. Adam, however, did the "manly thing" and replied, "Lord, let me tell You about that woman You gave me!" and that's where the ball started its long, unending roll. God then asked Eve if she had eaten the fruit, and Eve passed the ball along and said, "Lord, let me tell You about that snake!" (Genesis 3:9–13, author's paraphrase). And, of course, the snake didn't have a leg to stand on!

Theologically speaking, I know I'm in error when I make that statement. However, I am not in error when I say each one of us must recognize that it is not "his fault, her fault, or their fault"—it is our responsibility.

To solve the problem, we need to go back to the beginning and, starting in the family, teach our children responsibility. Next, we should pass the baton to the teachers in the schools and insist they continue to teach responsible behavior. Then, when our young people have learned their lessons well, they will practice responsibility in their personal lives and the workplace as well. When this happens, the responsibility crisis will end and we'll have a better society as a result.

*The price of greatness is responsibility.*

WINSTON CHURCHILL

# THIS IS A PHILOSOPHY, NOT A TACTIC

Fear—whether it is fear of falling, fear of failing, or fear of being found out—is a heavy burden to carry.

I frequently say, "You can have everything in life you want if you will just help enough other people get what they want." Here's a story that validates this in an interesting and life-saving way.

Dr. Bob Price sent me this little gem: One of the greatest success stories in the history of the United States in the twentieth century is the story of the Golden Gate Bridge. It was largely financed by Marin County and San Francisco, the two communities it eventually connected. Underneath the bridge there were two other "communities." One was a community of men working on the bridge, and the other community was composed of men waiting for someone to get killed so they would have a job.

Sometimes the wait was not long because during the first part of the construction of the Golden Gate Bridge, no safety devices were used, and twenty-three men fell to their deaths. For the last part of the project, however, a large net that cost $100,000 was employed. At least ten men fell into it, and their lives were spared. The interesting sidelight is that 25 percent more work was accomplished when the men were assured of their safety. The 25 percent increase in productivity paid for that safety net many times over. Not to mention what it did for the men's families and the men whose lives were saved.

Both communities got what they wanted. Their magnificent bridge served a wonderful purpose, and they got it at a much-reduced price because they helped those workers get what they wanted—a safe, secure, well-paying job. Think about it. Buy that philosophy.

*Even on the springboard to success,*
*you have to bounce a little.*

# LEAVE SOMETHING BEHIND

Mountaintops inspire leaders but valleys mature them.

F. PHILIP EVERSON

Each of us has been left a lot by preceding generations. Dr. Thomas Gibbs Jr. says, "Every man has leaned upon the past. Every liberty we enjoy has been bought at incredible cost. There is not a privilege nor an opportunity that is not the product of other men's labors. We drink every day from wells we have not dug; we warm ourselves by fires we have not kindled; we live by liberties we have not won; we are protected by institutions we have not set up. No man lives unto himself alone. All the past is invested in him. A new day is a good time to say, 'I am under obligation to accept my share of the world's grief, my share of its opportunities.'"

Life is a lot like tennis—he who serves best seldom loses. Responsibility demands that we pay our own way and leave something behind for those who will follow. Leaving a heritage of having lived an ethical, moral, and productive life is something all of us can do. Teaching someone how to read would enrich that person's life and enable them to make a bigger and better contribution to society. Acts such as giving a word of encouragement and setting an example of gentle kindness and thoughtful consideration for others are much needed in our society today and would leave your impact on future generations.

Unfortunately, too many of us labor under the illusion that unless we can do something monumental, there is nothing we can do. That's too bad, because doing something for others brings greater happiness to oneself.

*Parents: train up a child in the way he should go, and go there yourself once in a while.*

# FROM WEALTH TO BROKE TO WEALTH

## Opportunity is in the person, not the job.

When Castro and his Communist regime took over Cuba, the socialist system replaced free enterprise, and many successful people were devastated. Carlos Arboleya, an accounts officer for one of the largest banks in Cuba, was one of them. In 1960, shortly after Castro took over, Carlos arrived at work and discovered that the Communists had taken over all private banks. Three weeks later he was able to get himself, his wife, and his small son out of Cuba. The only problem was that Carlos arrived in America with only forty-two dollars in cash. He was unemployed, had no place to stay, and did not know a single person in Miami. He sought employment by going to every bank in Miami, but all of them turned him down. He finally found a job in a shoe factory, taking inventory.

Carlos worked with enthusiasm and with enormous energy as he put in countless extra hours. Results were spectacular, and within sixteen months he was manager of the shoe company. A short time later he was offered a job at the bank where the shoe company did business. From there he moved into the presidency of the largest chain of banks in America.

Carlos Arboleya did what he had to do (provide for his family) by taking a job he was overqualified for and eventually landed the job he desired. He proved that it is not where you start that counts but that you start. Speaker Joe Sabah puts it this way: "You don't have to be great to start, but you have to start to be great."

Carlos's story is a vignette in the overall picture of America. It's the land where anyone who will apply themselves and grow in the job can move forward to unique successes. This is evidenced by the fact that a sizable percentage of all millionaires in America are first- or second-generation Americans. Think about it, give it your best shot, and your success chances increase dramatically.

*My doctor told me that my appendix had to come out.*
*When I demanded a second opinion, he said, "That is my*
*second opinion. At first I thought it was your kidney."*

GARY APPLE

# MANNERS DO MATTER

*Gratitude is the healthiest of all human emotions.*

HANS SELYE

Today we too rarely practice good manners. However, having good manners, including expressing gratitude, is a great asset. When we neglect to require our children to say thank you when somebody gives them a gift, says something nice about them, or does something for them, we are raising ungrateful children who are highly unlikely to be happy. Without gratitude, happiness is a rare thing. With gratitude, the odds go up dramatically that happiness will be the result.

A classic example of the validity of gratitude in action is the story of Roy Rogers. After he starred in his first movie, he began receiving huge stacks of fan mail that he wanted to answer. However, his salary of $150 a week did not even cover the required postage. He talked to the head of

Republic Pictures in the hope that the studio would handle some of this fan mail. He was summarily turned down and told he was foolish to think about answering fan mail because nobody else did. It took too much time and money.

Roy Rogers, one of the genuinely good guys of life, couldn't buy that. It was his conviction that if someone thought enough about him to write him a fan letter, he would have enough respect for the person to answer it. Fortunately, the movie that caused him his "problem" also made him so popular that he could go on a personal appearance tour. He traveled many miles and performed countless one-night events to raise the money to pay the salaries of those four people it took to answer his fan mail.

As a result of answering each fan's letter, he built a fan base that was faithful to him and remains faithful to him many, many years later—even after his passing. Yup, the good guys and the good gals really do win. So develop some manners, respect others, and be grateful for what you have.

*I don't mind that my son is earning more*
*than I did on my first job. What disturbs me*
*is he's just six, and it's his allowance!*

# KEEP YOUR FINGER IN THE PIE

Leadership implies movement toward something
and convictions provide that direction.

DON SHULA

Former secretary of education William J. Bennett, one of the
guiding lights in the struggle to restore moral and ethical
values in our society, tells this fascinating personal story.
In the late spring of 1985, his wife, Elayne, who is a former
teacher, urged him to visit schools and teach classes. "While
we were still courting, she had seen me teach high school
classes in Portland, Maine. Later, when I became education
secretary, she told me, 'You're a good teacher and people
will take you more seriously if they see you doing what
you're talking about. In addition to talking about education,
why don't you go out and show people you can teach somebody something?'" Bennett resisted and said, "I don't do
retail now, I do wholesale." At that point Elayne persisted

and said, "If you do some retail, you'll do better wholesale."
Good thinking.

What she was saying is as old as time itself. By his example Bennett would be demonstrating the importance of and giving dignity to the teachers and the profession of teaching. Elayne was also saying that the real heroes of life are down in the trenches, doing the job and encouraging others to do the same.

That thought carries a message for every business executive. If executives are knowledgeable about every phase of their business, they will have a greater appreciation for what the rest of their staff is doing. Obviously, the CEO of a Fortune 500 company, or even a moderately sized company, cannot know everything about every operation. However, they should regularly explore what happens in each department and talk with the people doing the jobs. Not only will this interest bring them closer to their people, but the knowledge they will acquire will help them to more effectively lead the company.

*Don't expect your "leader-ship" to come in*
*if you're unwilling to unload the cargo.*

# TURNING TRAGEDY INTO TRIUMPH

Each of us will one day be judged by our standard of
life, not by our standard of living; by our measure of
giving, not by our measure of wealth; by our simple
goodness, not by our seeming greatness.

WILLIAM ARTHUR WARD

For many generations before the twentieth century, the
standard procedure for developing skilled craftsmen was for
the father to teach the sons his trade. The skills necessary
for the craft were passed from one generation to another.
Many years ago a shoemaker was teaching his three-year-
old son his craft to prepare him for life. One day an awl fell
from the shoemaker's table and tragically put out the eye of
his three-year-old son. Without the medical knowledge and
expertise of today, the son ended up losing not only that eye
but the other one as well.

His father put him in a special school for people without

sight. At that time they were taught to read by using large carved wooden blocks. The blocks were clumsy, awkward to handle, and required a considerable amount of time to learn. The shoemaker's son, however, was not content only to learn to read. He knew there must be an easier, better way. Over the years, he devised a new reading system for people who were blind by punching dots into paper. To accomplish his objective, the shoemaker's son used the same awl that had blinded him. His name was Louis Braille.

The saying is still true: it's not what happens to you; it's how you handle what happens to you that counts. I love what President Reagan said about his first term in office: "Since I came to the White House I got two hearing aids, a colon operation, skin cancer, a prostate operation, and I was shot." He paused. "I've never felt better in my life." I believe you will agree that attitude will propel you farther than bemoaning unfortunate incidents in your life. Give it a try. Take the advice of Helen Keller, who said, "If the outlook is not good, try the uplook. It's always good."

*One commuter to another: "Actually my mother-
in-law and I have a lot in common. We both
wish my wife had married someone else."*

H. BOSCH

# THAT IS MOST UNFORTUNATE

An apology is sensitivity and courtesy too late.

Years ago a unique service was started in Fort Worth, Texas, entitled "An Apology Service." The founder and creator of the service was Ms. Kathy Warman. For just six dollars, Ms. Warman would pick up the phone and, with her Southern charm and accent, offer an apology to the person you might have offended.

Unfortunately, there is no question that such a service is needed, but isn't it tragic that there is a market to have someone else apologize for you? Whatever happened to personal responsibility? It is inconceivable that anyone would be unwilling or unable to call and apologize for having offended a client, customer, friend, or relative. And regardless of how effective Ms. Warman might have been, there is a major difference between doing it yourself and hiring someone else to do it for you.

In most cases, the offended person is partially placated

by the professional apologizer, but surely he or she would wonder why the offender didn't pick up the telephone and offer the apology personally. First, an apology is almost always accepted. Second, it indicates that you are now thinking straight, recognizing your mistake, wanting to rectify it, and putting the relationship on a more friendly basis. Third, and perhaps most important, the benefit you receive from apologizing personally is dramatically increased. It means you have accepted your responsibility, faced up to a difficult assignment, gone through the process, survived, and even thrived as a result. Difficult? Yes, but it's a tremendous learning and growth experience.

Historically speaking, those who do the difficult things end up doing the easy things more effectively. Remember, an apology is often politeness too late. So think about it. The next time you've offended someone and need to apologize, do it yourself. You will have more and better friends, more and better clients and customers, and a better self-image as a result.

*You know it's time to lose weight when your mate tells you to "pull in your stomach" and you already have.*

# CAREFUL WHAT YOU LEAVE

The measure of a life, after all, is not
its duration, but its donation.

CORRIE TEN BOOM

I love the story told by Glenn Van Ekeren in his *Speaker's Sourcebook*. It was a hot, humid day in the middle of Kansas City. The eight-hour shift seemed especially long for the veteran bus driver. Suddenly, a young woman, apparently upset about something, let loose with a string of unforgettable, not to mention unrepeatable, words. The bus driver, looking in his overhead mirror, could sense everyone around her was embarrassed by the string of profanity. Still mumbling, the angry passenger began to disembark a few blocks later. As she stepped down, the bus driver calmly said, "Madam, I believe you're leaving something behind." She quickly turned and snapped, "Oh? And what is that?" "A very bad impression," the bus driver responded.

It has been generally recognized as truth that our first impression of a person is one we will hold for the longest time, and the last impression we have of that person is held almost as long. Political consultant Roger Ailes said that we generally make up our minds within a matter of seconds of meeting a person as to whether or not we're going to like them or even trust them. Those few seconds are important and will affect our decisions regarding that person for a long time.

One of the best ways to make a good first impression is with a smile and a pleasant demeanor. Yes, the first and last impressions are important, but over the long haul it's trust and character that determine the length and extent of most relationships. Think about it. Make good first impressions, make good last impressions, and in between be the right kind of person. You'll collect an awful lot of friends and admirers.

*Waiter to customer: "What do you mean the service is poor? I haven't given you any yet."*

# HIS COMMITMENT WAS TOTAL

It's true. Spectacular preparation always
precedes spectacular performance.

In the world of golf, many names are legendary—Jack Nicklaus, Byron Nelson, Bobby Jones, Ben Hogan, Arnold Palmer, among others. However, considering all factors, there are many who say that Ben Hogan would have to rate at or close to the top of the totem pole.

Hogan's accomplishments are too numerous to mention, but they include 242 top-ten finishes in PGA Tour events between 1932 and 1970. Hogan won thirty tournaments between 1946 and 1948, after returning from two years in the army. However, he is best remembered for the fact that on February 2, 1949, his car collided head-on with a Greyhound bus, and he was nearly killed. Doctors initially doubted he would survive. Next, they predicted he would never walk or play golf again, but just sixteen months later, Hogan was walking down the eighteenth fairway at Merion

Golf Club in Ardmore, Pennsylvania, putting the finishing touches on a storybook victory in the 1950 US Open.

His name is usually mentioned with awe, and people consistently make comments about the intensity of his game, his commitment to practice, his total concentration on the issue at hand, and his absolute unwillingness to settle for anything less than his best effort. He probably studied the game of golf more than anybody in history, and he worked diligently from dawn to dusk on the practice range, perfecting every facet of his game.

I know that you may not be a golfer, but I talk about Hogan because the qualities that make him a great golfer would have made him a success in virtually any field or endeavor. He had an unbelievable commitment and a strong work ethic. He studied the game as few, if any, ever had, and he had an absolute conviction that he would improve, regardless of the state of his game. I'm persuaded that if you'll adopt these qualities and focus on your chosen job or career, you will experience success.

*If you have a tendency to brag, just remember*
*it's not the whistle that pulls the train.*

O. F. NICHOLS

# THIS MOTHER IS RIGHT

Eyes that look are common; eyes that see are rare.

J. OSWALD SANDERS

Betty Stephans tells of visiting a friend whose three-year-old daughter frequently interrupted her housework by insisting that her mother "come outside and see." She would then excitedly show her mother a flower, a butterfly, a broken bird's egg, or a crawling ant. After the umpteenth interruption, Betty commented, "You're awfully patient with her, but all these little trips must nearly wreck your daily routine. Don't you ever just want to scream?" "Well," the mother replied cheerfully, "I brought her into the world. The least I can do is let her show it to me."

What a beautiful approach to take! How right and how wise she was. She gave her child a precious gift—her time. The housework will always be there, as any mother will tell you, but the little girl will grow and before you know it, she's out of school, married, and a mother herself.

Studies indicate that virtually all small children have vivid imaginations, but by the time they're ten years old, most of their imaginations have been stifled. One of the reasons is that parents either do not have, or do not take, the time to share the wonders that children see every day. Parents often fail to see that the stick-horse really is "a live horse in full color," or that the lines on the ground are a spaceship ready to take off. Too bad, because it's of such as this that little ones grow, develop their imaginations, and become the problem-solvers of the future. Think about it. Spend that time with your child. Let the housework sit a while. Otherwise, the little one might not.

*For some reason I didn't like that Disney movie. Aladdin rubbed me the wrong way.*

GARY APPLE

# IF THE DECISION IS WRONG, CHANGE IT

*If you have a dream, wake up and pursue it.*

The late Carol Farmer was an unhappy schoolteacher who realized after only two semesters of teaching that the education field wasn't for her. Despite her considerable investment of time and effort to become a teacher, she recognized that it wasn't her calling. But what else could she do? Her dream had always been to be a designer, so she set a goal to become one. Part of her goal was to make more money designing the first year than she had made teaching. She had earned $5,000 as a first-year teacher. As a first-year designer she earned $5,012, reaching her first goal.

She accepted a job with one of her clients for $22,000 a year, more than four times what she was making two years earlier. Shortly thereafter, she was offered a raise to $35,000, but her dreams had expanded and she turned it down to start her own company. She earned more than $100,000 her first year—twenty times more than she made less than ten years earlier and five times more than she earned the year before. In 1976 Carol Farmer formed the Doody Company, and in the next three years billed more than $15 million. Her staff increased from six to two hundred. She gained considerable recognition for her accomplishments and shared her business success with scholars at Harvard University.

Too often people see obstacles as roadblocks instead of opportunities. Carol took that calculated risk—which most successful people do (it takes courage to make the start, commitment to keep going, and persistence to get there). There is merit in calculated risk, but I'm not talking about gambling. Successful people don't take blind chances. They calculate their odds, which is what Carol Farmer did. In the process, she turned the disappointment and unhappiness of one career into happiness, creativity, and profit in a different career. I encourage you to join Carol Farmer in approaching obstacles and disappointments creatively.

*Money won't buy happiness, but it will pay the salaries*
*of a huge research staff to study the problem.*

BILL VAUGHAN

# CHARACTER MAKES THE DIFFERENCE

*More people fail because of flaws in their
character than for any other reason.*

DR. D. JAMES KENNEDY

One philosopher made the observation that if the immoral person knew the value of honesty, thieves and knaves, for their own self-interests, would become honest. You can check the record books and you will discover that all great failures are character failures, and the long-term success stories are people who built their careers on character. Most experts believe that companies have the opportunity, power, and responsibility to teach appropriate behavior to their people.

When character is taught in the corporate culture, the benefits extend into the family as well. Our own company has experienced this as we have persuaded the companies we train to permit the families—husbands and wives—of the employees to come in and participate in the training.

Results have been outstanding because it gets all the family members on the same page.

Katherine Nelson, a former senior fellow in ethics at the Wharton School, has said that there are three kinds of employees in any industry. Those she calls "good soldiers" know the rules and have a good moral compass. "Loose cannons" have a good moral compass but don't know the rules; they are full of good intentions but don't read policy manuals. "Grenades" have their own agendas, and their activities can blow up and devastate an organization. She points out that even "good soldiers" need steady coaching— and I like the word *steady*, to which I would add *consistent*. When we teach the entire company these basic concepts, we will have converted a group of wide-ranging abilities and backgrounds into a team that will produce good results.

*If someone offers you the world on a*
*silver platter, take the platter.*

WALL STREET JOURNAL

# BIG EVENTS DON'T ALWAYS GET BIG ATTENTION

*Doing ordinary things in an extraordinary way will assure you of an extraordinary future.*

Most people are familiar with the fact that on October 8, 1871, a fire broke out in Chicago, claimed more than two hundred lives, and destroyed more than seventeen thousand buildings. It has been sung about, and at least one movie has been made about that Chicago fire—not to mention hundreds of articles and thousands of news mentions.

But many people do not realize that on October 8, 1871, a fire also broke out in Peshtigo, Wisconsin. That blaze claimed an estimated fifteen hundred lives and scorched 1.28 million acres of timberland. Of course, the news media of the day were centered in and around Chicago, whereas Peshtigo was small and off the beaten path. Consequently, the attention was minimal. I think all of us would agree that the Peshtigo fire was significant, but because it didn't get the publicity, very few people are aware of it.

That's the way it frequently is in life. For example, Mother Teresa was world famous for her incredible deeds and commitment to help those who couldn't help themselves. She shunned publicity and made public appearances only so that she could encourage people to make contributions to the causes she dearly believed in.

Literally thousands of people are doing significant things every day to help a neighbor, a homeless individual, or those who do not have fuel to heat their homes or food for their tables. These silent angels of mercy do these things because they want to do them and because they believe they are their brothers' keepers. The joy and satisfaction of doing something with no thought of recognition, reward, or return are all the pay these unsung heroes want. They do their good deeds for unselfish reasons. Without them, who knows what state of affairs our world would be in? I certainly don't, but I can guarantee you one thing—it would be much worse than it is today. Be a difference-maker for others and it will make a difference in your life.

*Politicians who promise you pie in the*
*sky are going to use your dough.*

# HEALTHY FEAR

Fear God and you need not be afraid of anyone else.

WOODROW WILSON

There really is healthy fear. For example, it's very healthy to fear drinking before you drive. However, fear should not be allowed to run rampant through our lives so that it becomes such a devastating factor that it produces failure. The problem is not getting rid of fear but using it properly. Dr. Judge M. Lyle said, "Someone has said that the basis of action should be love and not fear. Theoretically that is true, but in practice it does not work out that way. There are legitimate fears. Fear of ignorance causes you to seek an education and fear of poverty makes you work. Fear of disease motivates you to practice healthy and sanitary living. Fear of losing your job will inspire you to show up on time and do the best you know how to do. Fear of failing a class will drive a student to spend extra time in the books. Fear of losing our family inspires us to be faithful to them, work hard for them, and show them love on a daily basis."

All of us should certainly have some healthy fear. There's real fear in walking across a busy street without going to the corner where the lights are arranged for that purpose. There's legitimate fear in driving your car at excessive speeds under any conditions, but particularly when the visibility is poor or the streets are slippery. We must learn to distinguish those helpful fears from the harmful ones. When you can do that, fear is a friend. Until you learn to do it, however, fear can be an enemy.

*True terror is to wake up one morning and discover that your high school class is running the country.*

KURT VONNEGUT

# GETTING EVEN

Among the things you can give and still keep are
your word, a smile, and a grateful heart.

"One of these days I'm going to get even with you!" is a statement most of us are familiar with. People are either threatening to or actually getting even with others. The problem with getting even is that we will never get ahead, which most of us want to do.

I love the story of what happened during the days of the Berlin Wall. Some of the East Berliners decided they were going to send their West Berlin adversaries a little "gift." They loaded a dump truck with garbage, broken bricks, stones, building materials, and anything else with zero value. They drove the truck across the border, gained clearance, and dumped it on the West Berlin side.

Needless to say, the West Berliners were incensed and were going to get even with them. They were going to pay them back. Fortunately, a very wise man intervened and gave entirely different counsel. As a result, the West Berliners responded by loading a dump truck with food (scarce in East Berlin), clothing (also scarce), medical supplies (even scarcer), and a host of other essential items. They took the truck across the border, carefully unloaded it all, and left a neat sign that read, "Each gives according to his ability to give."

The West Berliners had taken Booker T. Washington's philosophy literally: "I will permit no man to narrow and degrade my soul by making me hate him." The Bible says that when you repay evil with good, you heap coals of fire on the other person's head (Romans 12:20). In biblical times, heaping coals of fire on an enemy's head was an act that the Lord rewarded. It makes you smile as you wonder how the East Berliners felt, along with their gratitude for the much-needed supplies. I'm willing to wager that they were somewhat embarrassed at their own attitudes.

Message: Kill 'em with kindness. Don't return evil in like kind. Be more magnanimous than that.

*My six-year-old son just got a dog, so we're sending him to obedience school, and if it works out, we'll send the dog too.*

FAMILY LIFE

# HOW OLD ARE YOU?

*The most effective way to cope with change is to help create it.*

L. W. LYNETT

You probably know some people in their forties who are "old" and others in their seventies who are "young." I say that because I believe most of the readers of this book have confidence in the 1828 *Webster's Dictionary*. In his definitions of these words, Webster doesn't once refer to the calendar or the number of birthdays one has had. He defines *old* as "outgrown usefulness; belonging to the past; shabby; stale." I can't imagine that you would lay claim to any of these adjectives concerning the way you feel about life.

Webster says that *young* is to be "youthfully fresh in body or mind or feeling." That's the definition I like best, and at the risk of sounding immodest, I believe it describes me and the way I feel about life.

Ralph Waldo Emerson remarked, "We don't count a

man's years until he has nothing else left to count." I love the Old Testament hero Caleb, who at eighty-five asked that he be given the mountaintop where the giants were. He believed he could get rid of them, and he stated that he felt as vigorous and healthy as he had at age forty. Apparently, Caleb was right because there are no giants left.

Somebody observed that "a comfortable old age is the reward of a youth well-spent." This point ties into what psychiatrist Smiley Blanton said: "I have never seen a single case of senility in people, no matter how old, as long as they maintain an active interest in other human beings and in things outside of themselves." Personally speaking and relying on other sources, I don't go quite that far. But I do believe that, for example, that many illnesses are the direct result of a long series of wrong choices.

Follow sensible health rules and exercise on a regular basis. Continue to learn new things, fill your mind with good, clean, pure, powerful thoughts all your life, and I believe that you can live well now and finish well.

*Don't be critical of your mate's faults. It was those very defects that kept them from getting a better mate.*

# NEEDED—ONE MORE FRIEND

Life is an exciting business and most
exciting when it is lived for others.

HELEN KELLER

Somebody remarked that a stranger is simply a friend you haven't met. My trusty 1828 *Webster's Dictionary* says that a *friend* is "one who is attached to another by affection . . . which leads him to desire his company," or "one who has sufficient interest to serve another."

The dictionary definition aptly describes Mike Corbett who, along with his friend Mark Wellman, started the assault on El Capitan on July 19, 1989. El Capitan is a sheer rock wall 3,569 feet above the floor of Yosemite Valley in northern California. It is one of the most difficult mountains for rock climbers to scale. The combination of difficulty and danger is sufficient to test the strength and courage of even the world's most elite climbers.

It took Wellman and Corbett seven days to make the climb. They encountered temperatures of up to 105 degrees Fahrenheit and wind gusts that made the ascent more difficult. When they reached the summit, Corbett stood in triumph, but Wellman just kept his seat. Wellman is the first person to scale El Capitan without the use of his legs.

Wellman had given up climbing in 1982, after he was paralyzed as the result of a fall. From that point on the only rock climbing he did was in his dreams. Then Corbett convinced him they could climb the mountain together. Wellman certainly couldn't have done it without Corbett, who led the way and helped Wellman move through each stage, higher and higher. Perhaps the pinnacle of friendship and courage was reached when, on the seventh day, Corbett was unable to secure the pitons in the loose rock skirting the summit. Knowing that a misstep would send them both plunging to their deaths, Corbett hoisted Wellman onto his back and clambered the remaining distance to the top.

An old but very true statement holds that if you would have a friend, be a friend. I encourage you to be a friend as Mike Corbett was to Mark Wellman.

*The secret of managing is to keep the guys who hate you away from the guys who are undecided.*

CASEY STENGEL